Love of Beginnings

Winner of the Prix Femina Vacaresco and considered a masterpiece of autobiography, this is J.-B. Pontalis' lyrical meditation on his own life. *Love of Beginnings* exemplifies what psychoanalysis is about: passion, time and mourning, embedded in the flesh.

J.-B. PONTALIS is co-author of *The Language of Psychoanalysis*, founder and editor of the well-known *Nouvelle Revue de Psychanalyse*, and a full member and training analyst of the French Psychoanalytic Association.

JAMES GREENE is the author of *A Sad Paradise* (Macdonald, 1991) and the translator of *Osip Mandelshtam: Selected Poems* (Penguin, 1991).

MARIE-CHRISTINE RÉGUIS, a French analytical psychotherapist, lives and works in London. A member of the Arbours Association, she is in private practice, and teaches and supervises.

ADAM PHILLIPS is Principal Child Psychotherapist at The Wolverton Centre, London (formerly the Department of Child and Family Psychiatry, Charing Cross Hospital), and the author of *Winnicott* (Fontana Modern Masters, 1988) and *On Kissing, Tickling and Being Bored: Psychoanalytic Essays on the Unexamined Life* (Faber & Faber, 1993).

Love of Beginnings

J.-B. Pontalis

Translated by James Greene
with Marie-Christine Réguis

Foreword by Adam Phillips

'an association in which the free development of each
is the condition of the free development of all'

Free Association Books / London / 1993

First published in Great Britain in 1993 by
Free Association Books Ltd,
a company jointly owned by
Process Press Ltd and T. E. Brown
26 Freegrove Road, London N7 9RQ

Originally published in French under the title
L'amour des commencements © Éditions Gallimard, 1986

English translation
© James Greene with Marie-Christine Réguis, 1993

The publisher gratefully acknowledges the financial assistance of
the French Ministry of Culture in defraying part of the cost of
translation

British Library Cataloguing in Publication Data
Pontalis, J.-B. (Jean-Bertrand) 1924 –
Love of beginnings by J.-B. Pontalis.
   1. Autobiography
   I. Title II. L'amour des commencements. *English*
   150.195

ISBN 1-85343-129-X pb

Contents

Foreword

Adam Phillips

Autobiographies are always unfinished; unlike biographies they have to end before the end. The author, that is to say, with the absurd privilege of the writer, has to decide how to end his life. But how does one end an autobiography called *Love of Beginnings*? *'Infans scriptor'* , the last words of this remarkable book, suggest the progress of a life – from speechlessness to writing – but also remind us that language always begins from speechlessness; that there is, as Pontalis says with his inimitable simplicity, 'another space ... words come from that space, that it isn't language that makes language.' The exhilaration of fluency is always tempered by the sense that something else is beginning when we pause. *Infans scriptor.* The beginning and the end – or the frontier – that is always a new beginning: that makes the telling of a life inextricable from the living of a life.

But how many autobiographies make a life? One, of course, can never be enough. 'One shouldn't write *one* autobiography', Pontalis writes as a warning (and a promise) to the reader, 'but ten of them or a hundred because, while we have only one life, we have innumerable ways of recounting that life (to ourselves).' *Love of Beginnings* is not a psychoanalytic autobiography – autobiography, unlike psychoanalysis, can never be a profession – because of the author's eloquent commitment to the multiplicities that make a life; the fear, as he puts it, of serving one language only. So there is none of the jargon of modern autobiography here either (for which psychoanalysis, of course, is partly responsible) – no glibly revealing childhood memories, no smug repetitions or informed sexuality – rather a relish for the unexpected (what is a surprise if not the illusion of a new beginning?), and for the 'wandering' in language that Pontalis calls, for want of a better word, literary.

The story of a life is always, among other things, the story of a relationship with language. *Love of Beginnings*, because its title is not merely a confession, and its author not simply a psychoanalyst – he is also a publisher, editor and writer – makes an adventure, not a fetish out of his self-proclaimed 'love and hatred of language'. So the deft portraits of Sartre and Lacan – admiring, and without misgivings – also show us two sides of a preoccupation: eloquence as mastery and the impossibility of mastery; incoherence as mystification and revelation. If literature, as Pontalis suggests, is the enemy of the last word, then his unique but distinctively modern autobiography is the enemy of the exemplary life. 'What do we not lose', he writes ruefully, 'the moment we believe we have acquired our identity.' In this quest for what has to be deferred there is always an intrigued scepticism at work in his writing. In describing childhood not as what is to be remembered but as synonymous with memory itself, or in describing a fraught love affair, Pontalis is always after the provisional truths of uncertainty in *Love of Beginnings*: somewhere to start from again.

If Proust, in a sense, is everywhere in this book (but nowhere by name) – in the startling aphorisms and the elusive climates of memory – his perhaps inevitable presence is unobtrusive. And this reveals, I think, what is most enigmatic about Pontalis's writing; his apparently effortless assimilation of influences without any loss of his own distinctive idiom. Rousseau, Freud, Merleau-Ponty, Breton, Leiris, Winnicott – to mention only those of whom he has written so memorably – all haunt his writing. But they do not seem to have distracted him, so much as reminded him of his own way. Others have not been sought to acquire their conviction (that is, their style); 'everything', Pontalis writes, and it is the closest he gets to an article of faith, 'pulls me away from belief.' Disciples never learn.

'I like the fact', he writes, 'that the word "present" also designates a gift.' It is also a fortunate and telling coincidence that this works in translation: and that now both languages can share the gift of this book.

Translators' Note

The author has asked us not, on the whole, to provide notes on personages, works or places mentioned in the text.

Our translation was, like the Channel Tunnel, in an appalling state of *franglais* and confusion when it was read by David Black, Martha Kapos, Maxwell Shorter and Antony Wood: with their enormously generous and invaluable help it began to look as if it might after all almost reach England. We are also very indebted to Christine Cherniavsky, Colin Falck, Julia Henderson, Quintin Hoare, Anita Kermode, Alexander and Miriam Newman, Selina O'Grady, John Padel, Jean-Bertrand Pontalis himself and Manou Shama-Levy, who commented at a later stage. And we should like to thank Elsie Buckenham for her deciphering of the illegible.

Preface to the English edition

I am writing this preface at the same small desk, on the same island, where I wrote this book. The holidays have arrived, *vacances*, a word that for me will always rhyme with *enfance*, a time characterized by the recurrence of what is both natural and reassuring (trust based on the return of the seasons and above all of *full* summer), by free hours, by the rediscovery of immediate pleasures which make us believe in the continuity of our desires, in the simplicity of their object, in the guarantee of their satisfaction. I could very nearly say 'the long vacation', like a schoolboy when the academic year comes to an end, when the time-table with its precise and constraining schedule (but perhaps we like this constraint all the more when we fear the void, the *vacancy* of intervals, of dead times) stops regulating our days, stops cutting them into so many well-defined activities.

How regulated the life of a psychoanalyst is with its succession of sessions, week after week! How immobile this life is, in its enclosed consulting-room, in the hollow of a deep armchair! It may be idiosyncratic of me, but I'm often surprised to see my colleagues so little troubled by this state of affairs and the contradiction inherent in it: we who reckon that our treatment will be conducive to more freedom of movement, a bit more play and a bit less internal constraint, we (it seems to me) impose on ourselves a condition close to that of prisoners in chains – the chains of the transference; we are as if bound by a kind of physical paralysis only interrupted by timid gestures: the taking of a cigarette, the uncrossing of legs, the opening of a door only to close it again immediately ... We are pledged to experience only – but not always – a *psychic* mobility, and even that is always in the service of our patients. I don't mean by this, as is customary nowadays, to put in a bid for the 'suffering' of the psychoanalyst, his solitude, the discomfort of his position as an idealized or persecutory object, his function as a receptacle for all kinds of anxieties or as a dump for projections, the unease – to the extent of losing sight of his own identity – that the variety of roles assigned to him may induce. No, I only ask myself *what* it is we need to be on vacation from, we who are truly the only ones 'in analysis' for the whole of our lives? From what excess do we wish to be freed and, conversely, why, when summer comes to an end, do we hasten back to this impossible *métier* which is also our passion? Is it because without it we would be reduced to nothing but ourselves, to a *me* always the *same*? Could it be that our daytime sessions are the equivalent of our nocturnal dreams, the subterranean source which puts us back in touch with the infantile and, more important still, shows us the extent to which what we call reality is only a tiny sample out of an infinity of possibilities? No longer to dream is to be half dead, is to make reality one's only law.

The practice of psychoanalysis is both what prevents me from writing and what makes it possible. This book is the result of that contradiction. During the working

months I may write a paper for a journal in connection
with a conference, or give a lecture more or less related
to my practice, but I must have the interval of the
vacation, that is to say, a different time, a different
space – restricted but open to the sky and the ocean:
here I am on the island – in order to feel impelled to
write in a more wandering way, a way that (in the end)
has no other object than itself, a way that has come to
be called literature.

For *Love of Beginnings* is, if indeed I may be
allowed such an emphatic formulation, a work of
literature. I would in any case like it to be read in this
way and not as a document or as the testimony of a
French psychoanalyst. At no time in its writing did I
wonder whether I was speaking as a psychoanalyst or
not; I obeyed only one imperative, which, moreover,
wasn't formulated – that of allowing my voice to be
heard, and, if I may put it like this, heard by my own
ears: *my* voice, as if I feared, after so many years spent
listening to the voices of others, that I might lose my
own! The events reported, sometimes exiguous anec-
dotes, were secondary, they were written down, devoid
of any pre-established plan, following the flow of the
pen; it was this flow that led me, more than memory.
Events reported, as I said, or rather evoked (in
evocation there is a voice, a call to some unknown and
secret god) and, of course, when one is looking for
one's own intimate voice, one finds all sorts of alien
voices ... These voices in us are at once extraordinarily
distinct and mingled: the voice of an obscure school-
mistress may remain as imprinted, as present, as that
of illustrious masters like Sartre or Lacan; that of a

woman once loved, so elusive that she sometimes left
you speechless, side by side with another woman's
voice as you heard it every night at the end of the
telephone; that of a patient whose discreet suffering,
masked by irony, had touched me to the quick
resonates in the present as if I were still in a session
with him ... The multiplicity of voices doesn't come
entirely from childhood: I believe we are, fortunately,
never done with appropriating others, never done with
becoming *one's self's other*, but, at least as far as I'm
concerned, the voices are always linked to a place.
Memory is less subject to time – that enigma – than to
space, which gives it shape and consistency: a class in
school, a house with its garden, a hospital, rooms that
all keep for ever their particular smells. Our memory is
a *camera obscura* or, more prosaically, a box-room
where useless remnants hide, where blazing splinters
flare up: the disparate objects in a timeless attic.

The project of this book grew out of the suggestion of a
colleague: 'You studied philosophy, you were a pupil of
Sartre, a friend of Merleau-Ponty, a member of the
editorial team of *Les Temps Modernes,* then you came to
psychoanalysis via Lacan. Why don't you write your
intellectual autobiography?' Of that original prompting
very little is left in the final product, as far as
autobiographical purpose and intellectual log-book are
concerned. The initial intention almost immediately
took a different course.

Autobiography? Certainly this book, for those who
like 'genres', may be classified under that heading. Its
chapters are written in the first person, except for two –

which are, nevertheless, undoubtedly the most intimate ones — where a 'he' is substituted for 'I'. But it is an autobiography which, first of all, ignores chronology and, secondly, is very incomplete: whole parts of my life are not evoked, not even alluded to. 'Auto', certainly, but not 'biography': an 'autography', if you like, a scripture of the self.

And also, since I was convinced by the experience of analysis and, before that, by the study of history, that any story, however truthful it aims to be, is a reconstruction from the vantage-point of the *present*, I didn't concern myself with being 'objective'. I know that I haven't lied, that is, knowingly falsified facts or dates, but I have adopted the idea that memory is mostly a fiction, my fiction for today. One shouldn't write *one* autobiography but ten of them or a hundred because, while we have only one life, we have innumerable ways of recounting that life (to ourselves). This time I chose one axis, but without denying myself some detours, and this axis I've defined from the very first lines as being my relation to language (it may be that this book is only a personal version of Sartre's *Les Mots* ...) — a subject which could be judged 'intellectual' if one considers everything written on this theme by philosophers, linguists, essayists and more recently, above all in France, by psychoanalysts. But it has not been my aim, even if I had possessed the competence, to offer a contribution to a theory of language, of language's relational system *(langue)* or of speech-act *(parole)*. To put forward ideas, to propose and defend a thesis is one thing, and professionals are not in short supply to take that risk. But most often they are silent

on what has led them to their thesis, on their personal
sources and particular trajectory, giving us to believe
that ideas beget themselves and follow an autonomous
development. Now *that*, every analysis teaches us, is a
view that may reassure us as to the validity of our ideas
but that neglects everything to do with their genesis.
Our most logical theories are built on the same model
as children's sexual theories; only they sometimes
exhibit fewer signs of 'genius' (Freud's word). Before
becoming regular activities, my interest in analysis, my
taste for writing, even my editorial work originated far
back in impressions, passions and torments apparently
lacking any links with those activities; they are the
result of a process that was unaware of its own end.
Love of Beginnings retraces that process after the event,
and in a manner which I wanted not to be too ordered;
or rather it *traces* it, for a book is a beginning, not a
repetition. Perhaps, with the passage of time, the
original question 'Where do babies come from?' gives
way to: 'Where do our thoughts come from?'

Some readers – especially psychoanalytic colleagues –
shared with me their surprise, or even disappointment,
concerning the relatively 'classical' (to be understood in
the sense of not very innovative) cast of this book: a
mainly narrative form, an obvious concern to write in a
controlled way and so on, certainly a thousand miles
from the way speech is used in psychoanalysis. My
intention here is neither to plead guilty nor to justify
myself, but, beyond the particular case of my book, to
pose a question: is it possible to transpose spoken free
associations into writing – the sudden recalls, the

transferential shifts, the repetitions and the discontinuity of discourse? I don't think so. To seek to reproduce – to *mimic* – what we call primary process in a purported attempt at truthfulness is as artificial an exercise as the efforts of painters and film-makers to express our nocturnal dreams by means of figurative or cinematic images. Giorgione, to my eyes, is more dream-like than Salvador Dali ... Direct expression of the unconscious is illusory, immediate representation of a dream is impossible. Otherwise we should all be painters, we should all be poets. And let us not forget, at a time when there is lavish praise for the creativity of each and everyone, that poetry is a precise skill, painting a craft, and literature a style!

As an editor I have had the opportunity of reading numerous manuscripts by analysands who tried to stay as close as possible to the words spoken as well as the emotions experienced in the course of their sessions. However touching their sincerity, these attempts are a fiasco for the reader: they convey neither meaning nor emotion. The reason is simple. By linking the word 'work' to 'dream' and 'mourning', so much so that for us the words almost automatically go together – in a formulation that is paradoxical even if it has become banal for those of us who use it – Freud showed that activities apparently as simple and obvious as dreaming or as experiencing and then getting over a loss were no small matter. The same goes for someone who undertakes to write. Work, in all these cases, doesn't necessarily involve effort and difficulty, sweat and tears; it signifies *transformation*. The dream transforms sensations of the present, residues from the previous day, faces and memories, people and places: it is a laboratory. Mourning transforms the lost object, incorporates and idealizes it, takes it to pieces and puts it together again, and mourning needs time to do this. But as regards writing, the analogy isn't only with 'work': to write is also to dream, it is also to be in mourning, to dream oneself (and, for the greatest, to dream the world), to be animated by a mad desire to possess things through language, and to experience with each page, sometimes with each word, that this is never it! Hence the feverishness and melancholy, sometimes the one, sometimes the other, that always accompany the act of writing.

Analytic experience is not blind to such an alternation, and the points of convergence could be multiplied. But there will always remain a major difference: the speech that is authorized by the couch will never become an *oeuvre*, it is effective only on condition that it agrees to stray, whereas every writer, and even a non-professional writer such as myself, knows that he must constantly be attentive to the choice of the right words, to their tone, to the sweep of the sentence, to the rhythm, to the shape his book will gradually take. This is the price he must pay if he is to have a chance of conveying to his unknown reader something in which this reader may recognize himself.

To write is not in the first instance to express or to communicate, nor even to recount; even less, as too many scholarly critics of today repeat like parrots, 'to produce a text'. It is to seek to give shape to the shapeless, some basis to the transitory, a life – but how fragile a life! – to the lifeless. What both author and reader then hope to arrive at is not, as in the case of scientific writing, a conclusive truth or even a unique fragment of truth, but the illusion of an endless beginning. As long as there are books, no one, ever, will have the last word.

J.-B. P.
Belle-Île

1 Loving the lycée

I must begin with the H school. That is because it is there that I see the starting-point of my torments, at least of the one that will be my subject here: the love and hatred of language. I don't know if it's hatred or love that wins out; and I am undertaking this book only in order to grasp and recover – along whatever paths may open up – the nature of this passion that (I sometimes imagine) rules my every suffering, however apparently unconnected with it: anxieties of love, for example, grief, distress of mind or sudden animation – in short, everything that presents itself as a change of state. It may be that a single torment, always the same, displaced, misunderstood, is at the heart of all our torments, that everything which has some effect on us has one cause only.

So I must begin with the H school. Before, I had peace. There, I was on the rack. I was considered by my family to be almost mute, and yet I must have had at my disposal the few words required to obtain whatever was necessary: to drink when I was thirsty, to eat when I was hungry. But to open my mouth to speak – I didn't see the necessity. Mine was the state of *infans*. I didn't fall into silence – a fall which is often the only recourse of the adolescent; no, I *kept* silent: they said I was mute, and I wished to remain mute, as

if I suspected that once inside language like them I
would never be able to move out of it. I knew, with a
tenuous but stubborn certainty, that there is no way to
free oneself from that particular prison, from those
particular chains. At least one could win time, delay for
as long as possible the getting into gear. When I was
four, I used to imagine the jobs for which it wasn't
essential to be able to read or write, for which a few
simple words – 'Hi', 'Hand me the screwdriver' – would
be enough to sustain the camaraderie and get the work
done. I was attracted only by jobs that are assigned
nowadays to immigrant workers: I would be a dustman,
a labourer, I would wash people's cars. Since I would
use the same métro or bus every day to get to work, I
wouldn't even need to make out the name of the stop.

Such, for me, was the first baleful spell of language:
I could in effect be only an immigrant in it, a displaced
person; yet this forced exile gave me in return no
nostalgia for a native land. The handling of language
would make me lose the very possibility of representing
to myself what I'd lost!

But today my whole professional activity, which I
have tried to diversify, involves nothing but language:
I practise psychoanalysis, I edit books and a journal,
I read manuscripts, I write from time to time,
sometimes I translate. More than most, here I am
then: a man occupied, in different areas, with the
same subject – words.

Anyhow, at the age of five, I was placed in the H
school. This establishment owed its reputation to a very
special system consisting of several elements. I don't
know if in the minds of its creators – perhaps one

should say its engineers – the various elements of the system were deliberately combined. For me they were and have remained so.

1. We attended only once a week for a two-hour class in the morning.

2. At the end of the class we were given a short roneoed document, called 'the sheet', prescribing with impeccable precision the homework, exercises, lessons and reading that we had to do at home during the interval, guided, watched and instructed by our governesses or, for the less fortunate among us, by our mothers.

3. Mothers and governesses would attend the class, separated from the pupils by a flimsy barrier. They weren't allowed to intervene but sometimes expressed themselves noisily by means of sighs and exclamations, plaintive or indignant, in the face of our failings and blunders: 'He recited it yesterday without a single mistake!' Fans who wouldn't have missed one of our matches for anything in the world, they confronted one another, attributing our successes to themselves, complaining all the way home if we hadn't shown ourselves equal to the task. *They* were the children at the H school, moaning, vain, whining or happy about nothing.

4. The same mistress – for us, Mlle Haussoye – ruled from the eleventh to the seventh grade.

5. During the class we were taught nothing (which is why I hesitate to call it a class). What we learned, we learned at home, provided that we followed to the letter the prescriptions of 'the sheet'. The weekly session was actually a test and even a sort of exam. We were in fact graded at the end of each session into an order which

hardly changed at all throughout the year, and even throughout the years. We would separate after the announcement of the results, only to meet again the following week. We made our friends elsewhere. There, we had only rivals.

6. Things moved fast during the class-test-exam-session. Stragglers were lost. While, watched by Mlle Haussoye, we proceeded with the grammatical analysis of our dictation – the following year, as we already knew, it would be the logical analysis – her sickly young assistant (Mlle Haussoye was a robust woman) would be marking the arithmetic test we had just completed. While one of us would be reciting a fable 'with the appropriate intonation', another, in three seconds flat, distraught, pointing a stick twice his size, had to name that long sinuous line, blue on a green background, right in the middle of the silent map: the Creuse, Mademoiselle. A pupil called Cothenot had found the name: in a flash both the tributary and Cothenot were saved from nothingness. The golden rule of the H school: speed in speaking, in answering, in finding a rejoinder. To be caught unawares and to be caught making a mistake were one and the same thing. A bourgeois conundrum of those years: a servant who answered back was instantly dismissed, a pupil at the H school who couldn't answer back was incompetent, an idiot. Silent in front of the silent map, we would be forever condemned to the final state of mutes, of those who were retarded, kept-back. (Where?) Prompt, never disconcerted, handling the *mots justes* as if we had received them virtually as a legacy, we were destined to be diplomats, lawyers, captains of industry. And one of

us, who would be the representative of us all, would
end up as a Member of the French Academy. To my
cost – but I shall resist with all my silent strength – I
shall have to face the facts. Goodbye trowel, screwdriver and chamois-leather. How can one escape one's
destiny? The correct answer would be our tool.

7. I almost forgot: our supporters, as I said, would
gather behind the small barrier, but what of us? We,
sons (not one daughter) of bankers, senior Civil
Servants, industrialists and medical consultants, were
seated round a long oval table covered with a green felt
cloth, like a table at a board meeting or at the
reading-committee which I attend nowadays (once a
week and, I believe, on the same day). Such must have
been the certainty of the H school, the certainty that
kept its success going: once adults – which we were
already – we wouldn't have to change places.

8. All this still not enough to make competition our
absolute imperative, we were treated, in addition, to a
yearly exam and written work every term. But the exam
didn't arouse in us any apprehension. The examiner
was as debonair as his grey moustache. And above all,
through not belonging to the school, knowing less than
most of us about the pitiless rules of the game, his
generally flattering judgement on our performances left
us cold. As for the written work, it gave almost all of us
a chance to be first. We would write on the same
subjects as the pupils of a nearby state school, the Petit
Lycée Condorcet. Where the pupil who came first at
the Petit Lycée had got 16/20, the one who was first at
our school was given 20/20. That was a real godsend of
the H school: everyone who got between 20 and 16 was

placed first. Of course, this process somewhat disturbed
the ferocious notion I had of arithmetic and the even
sterner views I had about a strict hierarchy. I could
accept that one was first with 20, but how could one
still be first with 16? Nevertheless, what a piece of luck
for those 'kept-back', of whom I was one, and what a
comfort for their mothers! If ever they were forced
through unfortunate circumstances to send us to the
Petit Lycée, well, there we should be at the top of the
class without any trouble. Ah! how justified was the
word 'élite'!

And yet this dual marking left me perplexed,
revealing as it did a flaw in the organization of the H
school. If the marks were relative, so was 'the sheet'.
As for the small barrier and our places round the green
table, they were arbitrary, as were the grades that fell
each week from Mlle Haussoye's icy lips: 'First ...
Jean-Pierre Sautier' ...

Everything at the H school held together as in a logical
system. If one of its elements should wobble, the whole
ensemble would immediately lose its strength of conviction.

On my first day there I demonstrated my total lack
of understanding through a rejection, which in part still
continues, of the H system. This is what happened. In
response to the command: 'And now take your
blotting-paper', I immediately complied by pressing
with all my strength on the first letters I had just
written. It was the right move. But curiously, instead of
being absorbed, the fresh ink spread over the lined
paper: the sheets of blotting-paper were kept inside an
exercise-book, I had blotted with the cardboard cover.
This mistake, which was to be followed by many more,

filled me with joy instead of mortifying me. I would
attend the H school, since I had to, but I wouldn't be
one of the H school's pupils. Thus via my shapeless
ink-stains a combination was taking shape, a combination, in which I recognize myself, of compliance and
distance with regard to institutions.

When, some twenty years later, I read Ferdinand de
Saussure's famous proposition suggesting that every
social organization be considered as a system of signs, I
immediately thought of the H school. There I had been,
without knowing it, a semiotic hero, but an unhappy
one, an impotent rebel. Semiology would certainly
triumph, by definition it would have the last word;
without striking a blow, it would grab hold of its
predestined if not consenting prey: Literature. Then it
would spread to all the arts: painting, dance, architecture, cinema. Finally, our tiny everyday gestures would
be conquered by the imperialism of meaning: our ways
of sitting, of dressing, of taking our meals, of greeting
one another. But what about Nature? Wasn't there
something left there that escaped the ascendancy of
Language? We were still naively deluding ourselves:
what would what we call Nature be without the
imposition of names? By now there isn't a spot on earth
or even in heaven that hasn't been put on the map. The
H system, in advance, had given me a premonition of
all this: as soon as there was a map, the map stopped
being silent.

When I'm in a car, at night especially, all I see are
signs, I obey only signs, I emit only signs. 'Signal' or
'sign', what does the academic distinction matter at this
moment? I can then feel persecuted, the coerced victim

of those red lights, those indicators, those headlights, those luminous road-signs that prescribe my speed, my route, and tell me that I shall soon have, that I already have, no other existence that counts than that of a sign. But sometimes too I feel in subtle harmony with this miniature universe, I find a pure aesthetic quality in it: no corpulence, nothing superfluous. What if there were in all this an eroticism of appearances! Here I am, seduced: we are beautiful self-regulating machines, we are functional and vigilant. Moods are dissolved, disorders and stirrings of unknown origin soothed. What a delicious calm! But this conversion isn't made to last, it bores me, I want useless and above all clumsy gestures, I long for pauses, pointless exchanges, games without rules. It is in the indeterminate that I recover myself. What is strange today is that the claims of subjectivity come to be confounded with anonymous fusion. To get away from the frontiers of the great empire of signs our only recourse is to become, quite simply, a person in a crowd, to turn ourselves, without reservation, into a particle belonging to some mass: in sports stadiums, long queues, chock-a-block in the métro, swarming on beaches, a body for casual encounters. All in all, I prefer to be a pebble rather than a vector of signs. At the H school, where all sorts of codes were combined, of which I should have been the victim even if I'd had the key, I turned myself into a pebble.

Things changed altogether when I started at the Lycée Pasteur. What had burdened me and made me seek refuge in a kind of deficiency became a pleasure from the moment I entered that large red-brick building, where I was to spend seven years of happiness. Of all the slogans of May 68, the one most alien to me was: 'Lycée Barracks'. For my part, I discovered a form of freedom there. It had to do, I believe, with several things. First, I was away from my family, in which there ruled, as in any family, a secret law of silence. Not that we were particularly reserved – we even had our voluble members – but not everything that is transmitted powerfully among one's kin, not everything that creates attachment, fastening one person to another, hatred or love, resentment, discontent, can be spoken. A child perceives this more sharply than an adult. And should all this passion come out in the open, the effect, as can be seen later in couples eager for transparency, would be worthless. Only what is *not* said cements the life of families, a life that doesn't budge. At the lycée, in contrast, nothing was hidden, everything was said openly and, at least in my experience, said with the utmost fluidity; within certain limits, limits that were clearly defined and confirmed at every moment by the planning of the day, the internal architecture of the building: entirely separate playgrounds for the youngest pupils, the middle-school and the seniors; the time-table set for the year; the exercise-books; one's own class-room and waiting in a line in the corridor outside; specializations (in those days not very many: A, B, then from the age of twelve or thirteen onwards A, A', B, finally Philosophy or Elementary Maths); the grading of end-of-term awards (Roll of Honour, encouraging reports, congratulations); teachers and assistants whose whole career was involved in this; a precise distribution

of subjects, which gave our teachers a clear-cut task
and each of us a graduated sequence of obstacles to
surmount. Writing a commentary, writing a story,
writing a short essay. *L'Avare* at age fifteen, *Britannicus*
at sixteen. Physical geography, human geography, plane
geometry, then three-dimensional geometry. *Extracts
from Attic Orators*, and finally aspiring, with *Phaedo*, to
the immortality of the soul. The drawing class was
about the only one, in this rational progression of the
seasons, that was like a perpetual winter: pots and
lamps, then lamps and jugs. But one could escape it
without trouble: one skipped drawing as easily as one
was excused from gym. What need did we have to
balance stupidly on parallel bars when we were familiar
with the rather more delicate balancing of ideas and
sentences and knew how futile it was to reproduce the
poorest shapes of domestic life in charcoal, we who
each day mingled with the Great!

It shouldn't be thought that I'm yielding here to
some kind of nostalgia. There are whole pieces of
childhood that arouse in me neither regret nor
excitement. Or, if there is nostalgia, it's of a very
particular nature: as far as the lycée is concerned, it is
nostalgia for a world that was closed and minutely
ordered but – within this enclosure, within this order,
this regulated system – shot through with an extraordinarily open, fluid and varied life. Slogan for slogan, I
would say: my lycée was Versailles.

I found variety among our teachers as well as among
my fellow pupils. As for unity, that didn't require the
presence of a monarch. Through the devotion of our
teachers, who were so attentive to our progress, we
celebrated the unique excellence of the *langue*, of its

infinite resources for anyone who tried to master it, all
the while knowing the task to be impossible. That the
main teaching was of French, that we had, every day, to
learn a *langue* that we already knew made us, by the
same token, both unworthy and meritorious. Yes, I
suppose that's where I derived my model of a strict
equivalence *de jure* between thought and language,
between language and *langue*, and my ideal of a
fulfilment of the latter in its written form: a fulfilment
certainly subject to death, an indefensible and, it
seems, scandalous equivalence, but one with which I
never completely fell out of love. Nor with the worship
of the *mot juste*, which has already made me go back
over many lines of this story, of this scarcely-begun
essay (even though the canonical distinction between
'genres' is less strict now than then). Actors, seducers –
a class is held as an audience is held – our teachers
taught us hysteria. But, obsessional by vocation, they
were satisfied only by exactness. This exactness,
however – that's what the 'humanities' were – had to be
invented each time in order to be arrived at.

It wasn't the function of the rapid apprenticeship in
'old French', the prolonged one in Latin then in Greek,
even that in English, to upset our frame of reference by
transforming, if only for a few hours, our own *langue*
into a foreign one. It was the opposite. Certainly these
langues resisted us, as countries their conquerors, they
were not made like ours, faced with them we could be
totally bewildered, tears rising or some strange excitement that later we would be able to qualify as sexual,
but in the end there was nothing that wasn't in
principle, with the help of Gaffiot and Bailly,* capable

*Latin–French and Greek–French dictionaries.

of being translated. The red abbreviations in the margin
– cs., fs., md.* – were the proof of it every week, as our
corrected homework was given back to us. The
meaningless alone was infamous; the *mis*construction,
the false construction were only an indirect praise of
virtue; the 'badly-put' confirmed the excellence of the
well-said. The established supremacy of the translation
into the mother tongue over the translation into the
foreign tongue vouched for the pre-eminence of our own
langue: mastery of translation into the mother tongue
meant combining skill with an understanding of the
text; translation into the foreign tongue was only an
exercise in applied grammar. Berfougnat was the best
among us at this; we considered him a twit.

Suddenly, the natural sciences, such as chemistry,
seemed to me inexact. To make the litmus paper
change colour, what did that amount to? Collecting wild
flowers in a herbarium, a mania of the artless! I had
nothing against flowers, but to describe them dryly,
when they were already dry, to call them scholarly
names that didn't bring them back to life and didn't add
anything to them – I couldn't see the point. Even our
maths teacher had soon given us to understand that the
elegance of a proof was something altogether different
from the simple procedure used to verify the result of
multiplication – casting out the nines. So I concluded
that the only exact science was literature – in which I
included everything that had to be written in order to
exist – and that literature consisted of the authors in
our curriculum, and that history was Malet and Isaac.

* cs. = *contre-sens;* fs. = *faux sens;* md. = *mal dit.*

Still, let there be no mistake. Throughout my early years at the lycée my sustained reading-matter was the *Pieds Nickelés*:* their cockiness and vulgarity, their constant good humour enchanted me. So, agreed, it was more fun than *Polyeucte* or Cicero, I was therefore not utterly corrupted ... But I believe that I would have been even more delighted if they had conducted their swindles in alexandrines and couched their slang in oratorical periods. I would then have had the nobility and triviality of language at the same time, the splendour and the mockery of its acolytes. I was ready to pass without any hiatus from Ribouldingue and Filochard to Henriette d'Angleterre and the Prince de Condé. In the evening, in bed, aloud and for myself only, when my brother was asleep and my mother out, I read Bossuet, thus unwittingly putting the finishing touches to this education that I loved.

If there were no difference between a dead *langue* and a living one, or if the difference were only a matter of historical accident, I had to discover the non-existent and sovereign power of a *langue* in this funeral prose; and, since the gap between the written and the spoken was only a convenience, only the effect of our laziness, what better than this pure emptiness, this oratorical style that signified nothing except itself, to gratify me in those moments of solitude at night? I've never re-read Bossuet since – but I have loved Breton – as if this encounter at the age of twelve or thirteen had been enough to make obvious to me once and for all the splendid and sinister marriage of language and death.

* Heroes, and name, of a comic.

Between the child too long mute and the boy in love
with funeral orations, I don't think there was any
contradiction.

We had a lot of teachers. I've preserved all their
names in memory, and it wouldn't take much for me to
record them here. In my eyes they weren't equally
prestigious and they weren't all objects of love, but no
matter! What mattered to me was that they were more
than one. Each year there would be six or seven, and
each year (sometimes with one exception, which wasn't
to our liking) they would be replaced. That is to say, in
the course of seven years at the lycée, there were about
forty faces and voices, hundreds of verbal and gestural
tics, an infinite range of intonations, a panoply of
accents according to the province they came from. Thus
we weren't delivered up to the words of one teacher
only, we didn't run the risk of being moulded, wholly
fabricated, by him. (One could go on for ever about the
happy consequences of multiple identifications.)

Hence, certainly, my distrust of the Master who
assigns to thought the paths that it must follow, who
dictates to it his categories and his passwords. Hence
also my loathing for any official language, that's to say
in the end for any language that forgets its sources, and
consequently becomes domineering. No, what I liked,
what I still like, is a *langue*, a tongue, supple enough to
allow itself to be indefinitely renewed, to be imperceptibly seduced, to be diverted from the right path, docile
enough for nobody to feel a raging need to break it,
constraining enough for one never to forget its
otherness, so that, in moments of grace, I may be able
to merge with it and, afterwards, as if gratified by the

nothingness of words, recover myself. If such a tongue were my ideal woman!

On my father's side there had been bookish men. How can one know what they clung to most: their possessions, their library (*Revue des Deux Mondes*, books on law and history ...), their local political responsibilities? I imagine that it all made a whole and that they passed smoothly, those gentle dignitaries, those *cum laude* in life, from a session of the municipal council to the checking of their accounts, from the historical monograph concerning a local church to the sonnets they were writing in secret. But I have resurrected those ancestors of mine only belatedly. The great man of the family, who had the advantage of being alive and very rich, was on my mother's side: we were assured that he owed his success, his vast wealth, to his genius as an inventor alone: not one diploma, not even the *baccalauréat*, and everyone trembled in his presence. And here is the strangest thing in my childhood experience: this man, who (I'd always been told) was taciturn, shunning social events, expressing himself in curt commands or sudden fits of anger, was taken with a passion for words when language, in revenge, denied itself to him. When he became aphasic or almost so, he wanted to talk, he wanted to say things, and, for lack of words that wouldn't come, that wouldn't take their proper place, he would grab his interlocutor and not let go of him. I witnessed this torture on a few unforgettable occasions. I shall always see the narrow territory of words bounded at either end by the state of *infans* and the state of aphasia: Paradise and Hell, delights and torments, sweet sleep and

nightmare. Between the two, images completely ready to
compose a story.

Have I managed to show the difference between the
H school and the Lycée Pasteur, which marked such a
radical contrast in my life? I would almost see the
absurd and cruel H régime as the miniature model of a
totalitarian system and the lycée as the advent of
democracy! But it could be that, for the reader
unfamiliar with both, all this amounts to the same thing.
I am not overlooking what they had in common: élitism,
the spirit of competition, respect for ritual; in short,
everything that people affect to denounce nowadays
only to reconstitute it immediately. Yes, but at the
lycée, far from being subjected to the rules of the game
in their arbitrariness, I would see those rules as a game.
We respected the rules so that the game, thus able to
unfold, could bring us pleasure. At bottom, the bad
pupils were only bad players. And then we knew very
well that the game would end one day (hence its
charm): we had only to see the expression on our
parents' faces. We could also stop it at any moment, so
as to make room for other games. In the street, for
example, there were fights and toy guns, soccer in a
corner of the square, words of love dropped in the
letter-box of a film star whose address we'd found, later
there were three films, one after the other, on
Thursdays, if we ran from one cinema to the next.
There was, throughout it all, the game of comings and
goings: 'I'll walk you home. You walk me home.' With
the passing of the years, the chosen one could change:
dunce or first in the class, the dirty-story specialist, the
expert on the Tour de France, on jazz, on operettas

(Milaurie's aunt was usherette at the Opéra-Comique),
on *Paris Sport* (Legoul was a bit of a hooligan but his
mother was a poet), on girls (Lechassé had a sister who
gave parties), on running ... The lycée was a world on
the go, on the move towards the whole world! Have I
now made it clear that the ascendancy it has kept over
my memory also comes from the fact that outside its
gates we had a lot of fun, as, I suppose, beyond
Versailles, they frolicked in the fields? In order to live
and to believe ourselves free, we need several spaces.
What then is this servitude that I fear and flee?

The phobia of the prison of a single language ... I
can talk shop too. But psychoanalysis bores me to death
when it gatecrashes everywhere, when it affirms that it
is the interpretation of all possible interpretations. I
claim for one and all not a refuge in the uninterpret-
able, but a territory, with fluid boundaries, of the
uninterpreted. What is the good of inviting us to loosen
our tongue if we are then chained to another *langue*
which is moved by nothing but the powerful desire to
impose its word: you're not saying what you think
you're saying, you are what *I* say.

That territory where the unknown lives – but as a
nomad, a deserter – and which I believe to be our
starting-point in life, I saw it, later, treated with respect
by psychoanalysts who weren't from my neighbourhood,
such as Winnicott, mad about the child more than the
mother, such as Harold Searles, mad about madness
(without getting lost in or glorifying it). They probably
had to be far away, these colleagues, these elders, for
the encounter to work and to change them into intimate
strangers, a happy surprise to counter-balance the

depressing shift that turns our intimates into strangers. A tongue can speak, can go beyond itself, only if we're not too much at ease with it through having heard and practised it for too long, only if we feel incompetent to handle it altogether as a tool. Other and ours, let the *langue* be for ever our beautiful absent stranger. Briefly embracing, without being able to decide who captures whom, we have the illusion of holding her, but here she escapes again, suddenly recovering all her powers – of flight, dispersion, ubiquity, rootedness. Air, water, fire, earth: in a tongue, all the elements combine.

Philosophy, for a while, poetry – but above all when in fits and starts it erupts inside prose, without fixing its rendezvous in advance, without warning us that it is poetry and demanding our respect –, psychoanalysis, but only when it's not a treatise, had this effect on me of making the familiar strange. We perform our first and final transference on to a language that has always come from elsewhere.

One would have to recover – no, not recover, that's out of the question, one would have not to forget – that moment when men started to speak. For it *happened*, be it in a flash or a millennium. In this respect the experience a child goes through doesn't teach us anything, on the contrary it hides the moment from us, since the child has language at once behind him, in front of him and all around him.

As a boy, for a few weeks I had a taste for pre-history. Flint and bronze bored me as, later, the Merovingians and the Carolingians whom I never managed to tell apart. What appealed to me in these far-off men, my brothers, was, along with their animal

skins, what I imagined of their language: what could
have impelled them to speak? It couldn't have been a
need like the need for food or warmth. What then?
On that point I haven't changed my mind. I tell
myself that they invented for no reason, for nothing
that could have been of use to them, a *langue*
(simultaneously *langue*-language-speech) and that this
relational system, by necessity, was alien to them. It
had no connection with their gestures or their cries,
with their signals, with everything that already
enabled them to express themselves and communicate. It broke with their body. I would swear that
they didn't invent language to speak to one another
but to speak with the unknown: was that death? our
gods? They represented on stones, on the wall of a
cave, whatever they believed themselves to be
subjected to without being able to think it, in marks
that were not quite images nor altogether signs,
certainly not symbols. Words would be for later,
when the worst was over. First there had to be
language in the world, order and laws rather than
meaninglessness had to be communicated through it.
In these figures we think we recognize animals,
sacred objects, the phallus ... But we don't know. We
know that the advent of language cannot be known:
the question needn't be posed. We're only equipped
– and that's our strength – for describing, analysing,
classifying the processes of acquisition of what is
already acquired, for lighting up the way once it has
been cleared. And now that pre-history is becoming,
in its turn, a positive science, we're lost! We're no
longer going to be able to dream of our origins.

We're going to fail to recognize that language is only truly language, an active operation, if it carries within it what it isn't. I define that as the memory of non-language and I imagine it, just now, as one of those great working rivers of America, transporting trees and mud, mixing the desert and the sea, as one sees them traversing the thousands of printed pages of a novel by Jules Verne, in books that are red and gold.

Deliberately, angrily, I'm ignorant of everything concerning computer science. Where we're told of the triumph of a universal code, flawless, adult at last, ruling out all misunderstanding and giving us answers at top speed, I see only a cold hatred of language. On the computer, it's the shadow of the H system that, I've no doubt, is being projected. Like that system, this one too wants us, for our own good, to be at its mercy. It will kill the *infans*!

The H system succeeded in justifying my natural distrust of language. But the games of the lycée may perhaps have made the *langue* too loveable for me. I needed some time to unlearn both the loveable and the odious. Learning for me was, at every stage, learning then unlearning a *langue* so as to recover trust in language.

When I began to be interested in psychoanalysis, I could see no task more urgent than to make an inventory of its key terms. It was a homage to the lycée and my way of entering into a *langue* I could hear being spoken around me as if it were reality, a *langue* which had its users but had lost its author and, with him, any possibility of being an author in its turn: of begetting thoughts. I refused to be the user of that *langue*. I needed, at first, to inhabit it like a house we move into room by room, object by object, until we no longer know if we've learnt to move in it or if it's it moving in us. And then the second stage can occur, which is that of dispossession. Work on the *Vocabulaire de la Psychanalyse* had to be over before I could allow myself what is, I agree, an illusion: the possibility of thinking without words. But I consider this illusion to be necessary: without it, I cannot love language.

Outside the lycée – the street where I look, where I walk, where there are things and people.

Once the anatomy of a *langue* is known, its articulations disentangled, its nerve networks crossed in all directions, I only have one wish: to forget it. Failing the impossible – to speak a *langue* that would be only one's own and yet that everyone could understand – I fall back on the ordinary *langue* and I would like it to be violent and limpid like the sea where I swim in summer. I'm stirred only by simple words, and I see no other skill than that of transforming common into proper nouns. This invisible metamorphosis is pure wonder! As a reader, I curse learned terms, I hound neologisms, leaden words crush me.

I remember that after exams, as if to rid myself of the entire knowledge and above all the rhetoric acquired during the year, I used to go to town alone and there stop in front of things, nameless things: what was once perhaps a bit of pipe-work and could be a fish from the depths, a tree from the dawn of time, a man forgotten by everyone, a little boy asleep ... Eventually, from this fall-out of what had been useful,

from these fragments of pre-history, I would bring to
birth through metamorphosis the woman to come. That
was the time of my youth.

It was on my way back from one of those aimless
walks full of silence that I saw in a bookshop window
the title of a collection of Apollinaire's poems: *Il y a*.
From this title I constructed my aesthetic. To be able to
say just these words from before the time of words, *il y
a*, 'there are', and all things appear, from wherever they
come, they rush from everywhere, one towards the
other, they join up, they create the world. They speak
of themselves without our having to speak. Yes, he who
can say 'there are' has in one breath conquered death
and won language for his cause.

2 Angels and demons

On the table where I write, before my eyes, there is a photograph. The only one I ever wanted to put in a frame, not so as to preserve it better, for I would have kept it anyway, but, I believe, because it represents precisely what I made for a long while into the frame of my life. Is it necessary to add: the *imaginary* frame? A father and his son, a man standing next to a child, one hand resting on a shoulder. They're not speaking to each other, they're being photographed. They are looking at the camera. They loyally allow themselves to be captured by the lens that cannot strip them of anything. On the contrary, it's going to represent them, to make them present, together, for all time. This photograph became for me the very image of mutual protection, all the more so as it was taken in a place devastated by war and bears the marks of that: the ruins of a blockhouse, corrugated iron and concrete, a hole, an enormous crater dug by bombs. The son knows that he has a father. The father knows that he has a son. They hold each other. They count on each other. Together they are invulnerable. The hole is not for them.

Three days later, my father died. And, in order to keep my father, to hold him and hold myself with him,

once again I became silent. No longer, this time,
through a massive rejection of language, but in order to
speak only with him, in secret.

Silence of death to bring the dead back to life. The
only way to perpetuate the hand on the shoulder, the
shoulder under the hand. A belief in reciprocal
salvation: I was rescuing a father from oblivion, I was
rescuing a son from abandonment. Only a closed mouth
can preserve the treasure in the hermetic depths of a
body-soul. So as not to live out the mourning for my
father to its very end, that's to say (all things
considered) to the point of *erasure*, I shall always
remain, to a greater or lesser degree, in mourning for
language.

The words of those who remained alive were
therefore all suspect. Those people survived, that was
already not easily forgivable. Modesty, shame, simple
dignity should have prescribed for them an existence as
shadows. That they might live on, so be it, but
discreetly, with the volume down. The only interlocutor
recognized by me now being for ever absent, beyond
the ordinary means of communication, the living
exchange which I pursued with him couldn't be
achieved through words: rather, through dreams, which
are alone able both to deny and to accept physical
separation, to mingle appearance and disappearance in
an image; also through ill-defined states of mind during
the day, thanks to which I would feel at once alone and
accompanied, mortal like him, immortal like us –
together.

Soon I no longer needed this refuge, precarious and
safe like the hiding-place children find in the hollow of

a cave or of a hedge, a good distance from the home full of nagging. The pact of alliance, signed in secret and known only by the two interested parties, imperceptibly ceased to be in force. I don't know in what form it still ties me. I only know that I haven't finished with it. And when Guillaume was born, I did more than simply know: straightaway, again, I obeyed the pact made in another time and which I might have thought was over. The photograph, like an ex-voto, is only the visible, meagre relic of that time, the witness of a place of truth that was also a place of silence.

Since I could return to that place whenever I wanted to, I saw in the world of survivors only the reign of hypocrisy. And I wholly ascribed the hypocrisy to the pretence allowed by language, to its essential deceit. Language allows it. That's to say, it makes it possible, but it doesn't authorize it, for it claims to say what is. Alceste, as can easily be imagined, was the first of my cultural heroes. Like not a few boys of that age, I recognized myself in his denunciations. It wasn't men whom he hated, it was what men did with language, what language had done to them. That's what provoked his black bile. Only language had the power to make people ill and mad. Language or women: I suspected a disquieting equivalence there.

I could see the trap in which Alceste had been caught – which made him comic: why on earth had he fallen for a coquette, and one so quick to lie, rather than for a woman who would be both lovable and sincere? It must therefore be the case that, if she had been sincere, she would have stopped being lovable ... That troubled me, but I soon found a way round it. I

sided with the madness of the lover, I would have
preferred it to be even more uncontrollable and to be
avowed in its very excess: a continually thwarted but
uncompromising passion to wrench the loved object
away from the world ruled by fraudulent words. How I
was to suffer in turn, later, for taking myself, like
Alceste, to be the love-medicine! But, at the time, I
had one advantage over my hero: in the 'secluded
place', I wasn't doomed to solitude; there I would find
my father again, whose death had made him a fixture
for me, but not deprived of speech except to the ears of
the survivors who'd become, at one stroke, both deaf
and talkative.

Yet something bothered me about Alceste. A detail
apparently: the fact that he could only counter Oronte's
sonnet, which I didn't find any worse than some we had
to learn by heart at the lycée, with a song that I
considered pitiable and that, above all, wasn't of his
own making. Hence an anxiety: what if he too belonged
with the guilty ones? What if he were at bottom only an
incompetent Oronte, an invalid of language, in an area
where his more gifted rivals excelled? What if, more
than jealousy, it were envy that gnawed at him? It
could even be that he reproached the young woman for
her duplicity only because he was fascinated, in his
innate clumsiness, by so much grace, so much
lightness, and because he couldn't be an actor. Or else,
what if, in order to speak the language of love, one
needed a certain style? Mute, would I be able to charm
girls? Taciturn, I might attract but not keep them. But
there too I had an answer: yes, the artifices of
seduction could go to the devil but in order to abolish

them one had first to participate in the theatre and
undermine it from inside, with the aim of gradually
making their pretences evident to the actors. It was like
those 'Lives of the saints' that one of my pious
grandmothers had made me read: the story always
started by relating years of wild dissipation, of vain and
extravagant passions; asceticism would come later, when
the soul had been almost entirely consumed in their
fires. The only sanctity that had any value as
edification was that of the converted libertine. A born
saint was nothing but a village idiot.

One had therefore to surrender to the risky games of
seduction and language – in my eyes the same
perversity was at work in both – in order to be able to
protect men and above all liberate women from these
games. Since our innocence was lost, all that was left
for us was to attain another innocence, paid for with
our errings.

In the world, by which I understood the whole of
social life governed by rules and customs, there was
only one imperative, even if the codes of *savoir-vivre*
varied: to show oneself, to put oneself on the map, if
possible to 'shine'. I would submit to that without
balking, without – furthermore – disdaining the
pleasures that the strict observance of this imperative
would bring me; I would even yield to these pleasures
with a good grace, since I would keep to myself a
conviction that was to prevent me from being entirely
taken in.

To compensate for this sound wisdom that came to
me with success at school – success which we were led
to believe foreshadowed success in social life and

which had put me, without my noticing it, on the side
of Philinte – I had at my disposal an alibi where I
housed the truth. If, according to my plan, I could
respect the conventions of the world without ever being
fooled by them, it was because I could find the 'dazzle',
the incomparable brilliance, elsewhere, in a new
secluded place I had built for myself. That place
wouldn't be a thousand leagues away from the world
where one had to live, but right in it, in town, in
everyday life, which would be transformed by it. And
that place I assigned to love, to the loved woman, of
whom I had no tangible example around me but who
could be evoked simply by a look or smile exchanged,
without a word, on a bus or coming out of a cinema. In
these furtive, favourite moments, I would see signs of
recognition. Salvation was within my reach.

I no longer know now the shape I gave, during
adolescence, to this ideal hidden from everyone and
almost from myself. I only know that it was very precise
and nourished my dreams. But intermittently: a natural
reserve, a nature-reserve loses its *raison d'être* if too
frequented. The woman of my life, the one to whom I
would owe my true life and who would receive hers
from me, would be neither stupid nor mute, but her
intelligence, like her beauty, wouldn't need to declare
or show itself: both would be absolutely clear! God
doesn't have to prove Himself, it's men who exhaust
themselves proving that He exists or that He doesn't.
We, we *would be*. Occasionally our friends would spend
a moment with us, but I wasn't too sure whether they
would leave us convinced of the inanity of their
existence, of the definitive greyness of their affairs, or

whether they would be enlightened by the contempla-
tion of the glorious, radiant body that our union would
represent. And now that I confusedly recall those
fleeting day-dreams, I hesitate to see in them the
prefiguration of *l'amour fou* or proof that *Nous deux** is
not just reserved for people who live in thatched
cottages. After all, it's only a question of nuance ...

The fact remains that this visionary expectation was
as necessary to me as the pact of alliance sealed a few
years earlier with my dead father. No doubt it took over
from it. Now an alliance is always established against a
dangerous power; and it makes itself secret when the
threat is so insistent, so insidious and so diffuse as to
become hardly perceptible. It wasn't my father whom I
idealized, but my harmony with him. It wasn't the
woman whom I glorified, but a lifelong union. Two in
one, one in two. My father became my son without
ceasing to be my father. I became my wife without
ceasing to be a man. I visited the dead while staying
fully alive. And I was never alone in this world of
misleading appearances from which all truth was
absent. With my vanished father and then my
marvellous wife, we took up our abode in the true, as
others are in heaven.

I had received a Catholic education, more out of
routine and the obligation of our milieu than out of a
transmitted faith. It appeared to have little hold on me.
The weekly catechism sessions were a chore, I
considered confession an imposture shared by priest
and penitent. Only communion seemed to me – and

---

* Literally, *We Two*: a popular and sentimental magazine.

still does – an extraordinary invention. The slow,
dispersed absorption of that small whitish circle, of
unknown manufacture and substance and therefore
already ethereal, used to transport me. Where to? The
destination didn't need to be defined. The journey was
the whole metamorphosis. I swallowed a pastille and I
was a soul! I changed state, without losing anything; I
breathed in another world while continuing to move in
this one. What better to hope for, to dream of?
Afterwards, I found everything dazzling: the rain would
be sun, the road a field of wheat, my brother an angel.
I melted with generosity while the host – that mustn't
touch the teeth on pain of the whole benefit from the
operation being annulled – finished melting in my
stomach. During this brief moment of divine everlast-
ingness, I worshipped grey humanity.

I was all for communion in principle: since the
death of my father, the idea of redemption, the mystery
of incarnation, the aspiration to wholeness – and the
assurance that it wasn't out of reach – had won me
over. Yet I was suspicious of priests, whether icy or
unctuous, whose prosaic manner and musty smells
might put my private religion at risk by debasing it.

To go back along these tracks would lead me
towards territories that are no longer completely
unknown to me. But my intention today is different.
What have I done with these childhood beliefs?
Vanished in their original shape, where have they
remained active? One never gives up anything. Writing,
writing one's history, is exactly that: assuring oneself
that one hasn't really renounced, that across the
succession of dishevelled illusions the *thing in itself*

remains, that it has a life tougher than life! There's no
doubt: if I'd dedicated myself to literature, as I wanted
to do at sixteen, it would have been so as to dissolve
myself in it and save myself through it. I dreamt of
summoning every single word so that they would all be
erased, of covering thousands of pages in black so as to
end up with a blank white book! I would have been the
humble servant of this nocturnal light.

This alliance outside time, this ideal union, this
waiting for the concert of passion from which all
disharmony would be banished – all this *elsewhere*
imagined and celebrated as the place of truth, the
refuge of the in-itself – had its reverse side. I was also
in the hands of two demons. Equally imaginary, they
represented my real world, they were its sinister
ambassadors. Hence their power and their constancy.

I had to call forth my day-dreams (as one has
recourse to an image) in order to give life to pleasure,
whereas these demons would intervene without warning, they set the appointment themselves and would
appear before me when I least expected them. As best I
could, I gave them a name, if only so as to identify
them: demon of the 'nothing to say' and demon of the
'familiar'. In an attempt at exorcizing their deleterious
powers, I gave them different names but I knew them to
be brothers. They defined my reality, these demons of
the immobile.

The 'familiar': that was the furniture, the objects,
the walls, the Rue Perronnet which I walked along
every morning, the metal shutters closed every night,
the disused garage opposite our ground-floor flat, the
fixed times for meals, my mother's small steps, her

permanent sadness, the stubbornness of things –
whatever is the way it is, whatever doesn't budge,
whatever stays in place, there where it's been put.
No, not everything that stays in its place, for the
immobile has two faces. There is one of them that
reassures, such as the return of the seasons which
leads one to believe that the rhythm of human life
also escapes the passage of time, such as the coffee
drunk at the counter before going to work, such as
the dog who will sleep only on that cushion ... I need
this guarantee of continuity. The other, overwhelming
aspect, I would find it and still do when, for
instance, back from a journey, the ashtray that I
forgot to empty before I left has retained its cigarette-
ends, when the manuscript I stopped reading, from
tiredness or boredom, is still open at the same page
... Ah, these remains of the remains of us, this
perpetuation of scraps, this endless fall-out of what
was once alive! That is doubtless what my demon of
the familiar would whisper to me in a voice which
was by turns suave and sarcastic. He appeared in my
life at the time when I believed childhood was going
to abandon me, when the familial, so I also believed,
was going to stop weighing me down, when I was
beginning to feel myself free as regards my movements, my tastes and my choices. While I would
experience in flashes this vague but exhilarating
feeling of being born to myself, the demon would
spoil everything and call me back, with no beating
about the bush, to the order of things. To challenge it
– I remember this winter, the first one of the
Occupation, when, badly fed, with hardly any heat,

we would keep our pullover and socks on in bed – I stupidly decided to change the position and orientation of everything in my room, having first got rid of anything superfluous. The armchair was therefore placed on top of the wardrobe, the shutters stayed shut during the day, the spines of books were turned to the wall, offering to the gaze their greyish and idiotic bellies only; I slept on the floor, I went out in the cold in shirt-sleeves ... The cure of a deliberately impoverished imagination, a derisory badge of derision. Wanting thus to turn the world upside down within the narrow confines of my room, I wasn't trying to be provocative. It was only another way of subjecting myself to the hold of the familiar. That's all I can do, which is nothing, I was saying to the demon, you're stronger, you've won.

A severe-looking physics teacher had, a few months earlier, written out on the blackboard in the following words the second principle of thermodynamics: 'Nothing gets lost, nothing gets created, everything runs down.' The window of my room had become this blackboard. Nothing gets lost, nothing gets created, everything runs down, such was the formula of my melancholy.

It was the same movement of impotence and defeat faced with the weight of things – this weight that at once kept them eternally present and engulfed them in irreversible deterioration – which also made me yield to the even greater powers of the brother-demon, him of the 'nothing to say'. He revealed to me the negative face of silence, as unhappy as words. To keep quiet, to speak, was all one. Between keep-talking and mouth-shut-tight, where was the choice? When language can achieve nothing, silence is leaden.

At the time, fortunately quite brief, when my two demons were visiting me, I did have an inkling that they were in alliance: too much of the 'familiar' necessarily called forth the 'nothing to say'. But I didn't see that they were only the obverse – the deadly, destructive representation – of my earlier beliefs: the invisible pact of alliance with my father, the visible at-one-ness with the woman. Angels and demons, as one would say today, 'made a system'. To stop being possessed by either, I had to discover a language that would give me the illusion of possessing – not outside language, but thanks to it. That's what the philosophy class gave me.

3 The taking of speech

He stood out. Was it because of the (dry) voice, the (cutting) words, because of the rumours circulated (to the effect that he didn't wear a tie)? The fact is, he stood out. I knew it the moment I went into the class-room that morning, slightly late. He was there without our having been told he was coming back, so that for a second I thought I was in the wrong room. 'A factual judgement concerns what is. A value judgement concerns what ought to be.' These were, I believe, his first dictated words. It was Spring 1941 and we were beginning 'Ethics' ...

Before that, for months, we had been gently rocked by the soft Bergsonism of Monsieur Charlier. While boasting to us of the infallibility of the instinct of sphex (which I never heard of again, does it even exist?), he was for the hundredth time breaking the frame of his spectacles. Without even noticing it, he would continue. What if, for a philosopher, I said to myself, instincts were thoughts and speech were automatism? M. Charlier's sentence was thus uninterrupted, there was always only one sentence, from one day to the next, from one chapter to the next. I liked this man, a bit dirty and puffed-up, physically awkward, whose discourse knew neither beginning nor end. He embodied *la durée*. With him the lump of sugar never finished melting ... That was reassuring to me in those days

when time had just fractured – for ever, I believed: I
couldn't conceive of an after-the-war, rather *the end of
the world*; it was comforting to feel that, underneath, I
could have access to that duration which distanced the
horror of the present.

'To sleep is to lose interest ... as Bergson says.'
Vaguely sleepy and, suddenly, convinced that we were
profound since, in that state, we discovered ourselves
naturally attracted to our internal worlds, we floated,
carried along by his liquid speech. Certainly we knew,
even though our teacher – with such sadness! –
celebrated the virtues of the 'creative imagination', that
all he would do would be to reproduce each year this
same course which didn't teach anything. But that was
also reassuring: philosophy was therefore not a question
of knowledge but, literally, of disposition of mind. It
was enough to clear a little room for the Mind which,
during the process of clearing, acquired a capital, and
then it became possible to assimilate the whole world ...
Was M. Charlier dull, sad, confused? Were his courses
insubstantial and their traces immediately erased?
What did it matter to me? He brought within my reach
a precious good, completely new for me: language, even
poorly mastered, and whatever its weakness, could
solve everything. Yes, that is what philosophy, as it
flowed from his malleable lips, was for me at first: like
an immense paraphrase of the real world. One could
disappear into that philosophy.

With Sartre (for he it was – the outstanding,
trenchant man), everything totally altered. The mutation
came without warning. I was at ease in what was
imprecise. I appreciated in M. Charlier that he never

opposed doctrines, put forward theses, that going from
dream to memory, from the psychophysiology of
sensation to mathematical reasoning, was a single route,
a landscape of soft transitions which the gaze never
mastered but where it wouldn't get lost either. All we
encountered, in scarcely differentiated, discreetly hier-
archical shapes, were manifestations ... of what exactly?
Of Consciousness, of Life, of Mind? That too remained
undetermined, a big X of which it was enough for us to
know that it was there, a halo of mist on the
landscape's horizon. Always behind in the curriculum,
M. Charlier would find a way of sketching for us its
outlines a few days before the *bac*. That was probably
what was called Metaphysics. I was being gradually
impregnated by a mixture of clarity and mystery. A
philosopher had probably nothing to say but he could
gently assimilate everything. In so doing, he would
never break anything except a few side-pieces of his
spectacles. Why not become in my turn a teacher of
philosophy?

And now the little man – who was wearing a tie and
even, if I remember correctly, a three-piece suit! – was
going to tear me recklessly away from this pleasant
torpor, from this glazed trust. At a distance of so many
years, and especially because of what I discovered
about him later, I couldn't say exactly how it worked. I
only know that I resisted at first, aware of what I was
going to lose and having the feeling that some immense
task might then become my responsibility, mine and
everyone else's. I couldn't see clearly what that task
would be, but it was enough to hear the cutting voice to
know that I wouldn't easily find excuses in inertia – the

inertia of the familiar, of the family, of dead time.
Inertia and its principle could indeed rule the order of
things, but I would no longer find in them anything to
exonerate my apathy. This man, it was obvious, didn't
tolerate the vagueness of states of soul: there was no
room in him for either the vague or the state or the
soul. He also – drily – challenged vagueness of
thought. Nothing was assimilable but everything was
intelligible. And if everything was intelligible, submission to a putative law of reality was called self-
indulgence. Eight days after Sartre's arrival, with a
school-friend I pulled down Marshal Pétain's photograph pinned on the class-room wall ... I needed time
to see the difference between a gesture and an action.

During those months, Sartre didn't say a word to us
about Vichy and the defeat, not a word about the Stalag
he had come from. But he set us as the subject for an
essay: 'Remorse'. It was only when I saw, two years
later, a production of *Les Mouches* that I understood
that choice. At the time, I had found it disconcerting:
Sartre and remorse, they didn't go together.

Today it's difficult to utter the name 'Sartre' without
immediately conjuring up an overpowering image. In
1941, there weren't many of us who knew, with
absolute certainty, that he was Sartre. Where does this
feeling of unmistakability come from? It's a rock, it
comes only from itself. It doesn't seek to be communicated, it doesn't seek to justify itself, it might rather –
to others – appear to be a secret: there are only a few
who know, who own this fact but, even among those
who know, it's not mentioned. Driven into a corner,
forced to provide proofs, we would only have been able,

with bad grace, to invoke the ontological argument, but
the other way round: Sartre exists, therefore he is! I
had liked, as I said, some of my teachers, but certain
signs showed me that this liking was entirely due to the
situation, was located in it, and would vanish into thin
air outside it, outside the closed world of the lycée: the
lycée was my love-object, the teachers were only its
emanations. A similar phenomenon occurred with the
brief passions I experienced for people met on holiday,
which vanished when I got back to Paris. The 'gang'
once disbanded, the seaside loves had flown away!

I didn't see Sartre as a teacher, I didn't limit him to one
function, he referred only to himself. None of the words –
respect, admiration, fascination – would be appropriate
here. Yet I turned him into something like my god.

It's firstly because I found a complete harmony
between what Sartre said and the person he was. For
several weeks he explained to us Kant's ethics, but it
was Sartre who was speaking, as if Kant's thought were
taking shape directly in his own head and in front of
us, as if he were giving that thought existence in
recounting it. I imagined – and in fact I wasn't far off –
that faced with any object, even and especially the
most trivial, it would have been the same. He would
consider it for a while, like a roofer surveying the heap
of tiles he's going to turn into a roof, before saying to
himself 'Let's go' and going. Small of stature, but with a
solid body, he was a mental manual worker, a
proletarian of existential consciousness. And it wasn't
the worthiness of the material that assured the interest
of the work. Anything would do: a loaf of bread, a bus,
'my friend Pierre' (that last one had me really

wondering!), an angry man, the waitress in the restaurant. With M. Charlier, with books, I had ended up thinking that to be a philosopher it was enough to go through two simple operations: first, to choose an abstract term, then to label it 'idea', like putting the particle *'de'* in front of a common name. To discourse on nature would have been staying inside Literature; to meditate on the *idea* of Nature, that was already philosophizing. When we were able to hold together Man and Nature in their antagonism, we would have earned our stripes as dialecticians. Philosophy was a noble activity guaranteed by the nobility of its objects.

When Sartre took the métro, I imagined that he asked himself the question: 'What exactly is the métro?' – the damp heat, or a tired face? – just so as not to stop thinking. Sartre falling asleep, that was inconceivable! If, on holiday, he contemplated a landscape, it certainly wasn't to melt into it gently as I liked to do, or if so he would turn this brief melting into a component of the landscape's *essence*. I never said to myself in front of Sartre: 'He knows so many things!' nor wondered: 'Where does he get it all?' I would note, usually with elation, sometimes with a certain terror: everything can be said then, so long as one wants it to be. The proposition 'everything has a meaning' – that by now has become so flat, so loaded with boredom that it destroys delight – was at first, for me, coming from where I came from, an exhilarating programme. Experience itself wasn't necessary. Sartre, I would have sworn, had never been water-skiing, and yet he could describe – page after page – the enjoyment of the skier. Ah! how *carefree* intelligence could be!

Yes, Sartre had a free and easy intelligence, a skiing one – *schuss* and *slalom* – but he sometimes made mine seem sad and pedestrian: I wasn't sure that I was up to it! Even today there's a form of intelligence that makes me envious and horrifies me at the same time, an intelligence that never has an appointment except with itself, is ignorant of its own trajectory, misunderstands its own folly: the indefatigable, conceited producer and consumer of 'ideas'. Faced with *les beaux esprits*, I run away: Alceste isn't dead ... And with him the stupid, insistent, stubborn question springs up along with a retreat from words that are too glib: it's sparkling, it's ingenious, the wheels go round, the machine functions, it's productive, but is it true? It keeps together, but does *it keep* to reality, to that substance of things with which it must, in the end, join up? The work of the painter's hand in front of a live model, in his attentiveness, his patience, his tireless re-touching, his minute and precise movements, from the palette to the canvas, will always seem to me less suspect than that of the hand with a pen.

It's above all when I want to write on psychoanalysis, to attempt to convey what I actually encounter in it, that this dissatisfaction, this anxious passion takes hold of me. For it's then not a matter of observing facts nor of inventing stories. I don't have to provide evidence for what I propose and yet I must make it convincing. The object isn't offered to the gaze and yet it exists. How then make it perceptible to the reader, how make him, in turn, recognize this object in himself, this object which never allows itself to be seen, to be caught, which never lets itself be glimpsed head-on? Session after session, these recumbent men and women

recount the images that hold them, excite them or over-
whelm them. To alleviate their surrender, we analysts – men
seated, women seated – want to give them something other
than words: this *seat*, to be precise, this basis for judgement,
this 'assize', without which there's no freedom of movement
– rather, exhausting turmoil or deadly stagnation. My ideal
as analyst: to be the one who *keeps his word*. I trust this
exchange – it has its *raison d'être* in itself, it isn't sapped by
the 'what's-the-point?' – but I would like to be able to
communicate what in it is clear, to convey its modalities
which remain, let's face it, widely unknown. I would like to
do better than telling of this exchange, for telling what's
already been told in thousands of ways is always only
re-telling. A dream: to be able to paint the unheard-of!
Paint, not translate. The power of an art resides in
confronting what negates it: music confronting the visible,
literature silence. Why did I become a psychoanalyst if not
endlessly to measure language against what it isn't?

I later considered Sartre to be, if not totally
overcome by the madness of words, at any rate, in the
exhausting struggle he always fought against it,
inclined, with the help of corydrane,* to yield to this
madness. But, at the time in which I am now trying to
locate myself, in that year when he came into my life,
his strength in my eyes came from this: he was able,
and without posing but straightforwardly, to think what
I believed to be outside the boundaries of thought, he
was able to name what seemed to me inaccessible along
the paths of language. Even more: to say what it was
that prevented me from speaking, what forbade me to

* A stimulant.

speak. The weight of things. Yes, things had a weight, but that alone guaranteed a weight to speech. Otherwise speech would have been so much hot air. Each generation, no doubt, has this experience: of encountering a literature which makes everything else appear to be literature ... Ah, the meditation on the pebble, on the root of the tree in the park. My demon of the 'familiar' was suddenly exorcized: far from summoning his acolyte, the 'nothing to say', far from paralysing, he made speech possible. He was at the origin of words. In one shot, I went from *Les Nourritures terrestres*, of which I knew some passages by heart, to *La Nausée*, whose every line I made mine. And it was Roquentin who was teaching me ardour, and the fragile Nathanaël who nauseated me. It was like an enlightenment: I could see through the murk, I named the unnameable, the mournful Rue Perronet acquired a metaphysical dignity. Living by mistake in Neuilly, I lived in fact in Bouville, each week I 'fucked' Mme Moutier, the enticing mother of my class-mate, at the Hôtel du Commerce. In the bourgeois of the Côte, I could, stretching it only a little, recognize my family; in the Autodidact, the good pupil, foolish and touching, that I might have been for ever. And the day when I discovered 'Some of These Days' in a shop on the Rue de l'Odéon – for now I walked through the city alone – I lived a *moment parfait*.

If Sartre's intention in *La Nausée* had been to denounce salvation through art, the result for me was the opposite: literature transformed existence, and only naked existence could bring forth a literature that might not be pretence. By plunging into things, it

would release ... what? Their meaning, their meaninglessness, it was all the same, since things were
simultaneously other and sayable. At the end of the
operation, if it were successful, the pebble would be
transformed into a book and the book into a pebble. By
refusing to be an artist, the writer − and everyone could
be one − realized this miracle of art: to create a *thing*!
Thinking authorized bizarre practical consequences:
since adventure was a masquerade (Sartre had settled
that in a way I considered a bit expeditious but which
suited me fine), I was a little old man slowly sipping
not a glass of absinthe but a bouillon cube on a
worn-out imitation-leather chair, a true character from
a novel; hanging around at the race-course in Auteuil −
an indirect homage to my father who had volatilized
considerable sums there − I was transformed into a
lucid hero of the absurd.

Lucidity! It was my key word, but there was no need
to utter it. That would have been elevating it to the
level of cardinal virtue when, as I was fully determined
never again anywhere to be a good little boy, I thought
I had nothing to do with virtue. Besides, hadn't
Roquentin dealt humanism blows from which I thought
it wouldn't recover? What exactly did I mean by
'lucid'? With respect to others, that wasn't much of a
problem: a distant, critical gaze was enough to protect
me from the traps of the 'serious'. I had exulted,
reading *La Nausée*, in the portrait gallery at the
Museum: there was no good reason to hate those
conceited men and those saintly women, one had only
to look at them for them to be as they appeared to be.
No sarcasm, just a look. Later, I liked the mixture of

ferociousness and generosity in Sartre: biting and with
an open purse, who can do better? Lucid, not fooled,
even merciless, towards others, yes of course. But
towards oneself? That wasn't so simple. Certainly,
Sartre offered me one recourse: he explained to us, or I
had read it in his books, that one 'chooses' to be angry
and even to faint, that one 'decides' on the moment
when one's too tired to climb that rock; and that one
could just about fall in love if one wanted to ...

Nevertheless I found it very difficult to recognize
myself in these analyses, which imposed a freedom
without limits. On the whole, was it better to know
oneself to be free at every moment rather than entirely
determined? Scarcely able to refute such a radical
thesis with arguments, even accepting its rightness as
far as the behaviour of others was concerned, I couldn't
find myself in it: I couldn't find there all those
moments at once powerful and fleeting, alternately
painful and luminous, and consequently disconcerting,
in which the 'I' that Sartre always seemed to appeal to
as a prop, this *I* without contents yet ubiquitous, was
lost. Where had it gone to? Where did it come from?

Those moments could be the continuation of a dream
whose images I had forgotten but whose effect remained
perceptible all day, colouring all my activities with
sadness or desire; or a feeling of vacuity, of wandering,
when, for instance, a gap unexpectedly opened up in
my time-table and called forth nothing in response but
my own vacancy. Certainly, I could see, agreeing with
Sartre, that in a way I 'decided' to experience fully
these moments of vacillation, of vertigo, instead of
brushing them off with the back of my hand. But that's

because I felt there was something precious in them: I had to cross these murky waters; I had to take into account these unclear messages from a far-away and unknown place if I didn't want to reduce myself to being a frozen head. That's perhaps what has kept me, through the years, at a certain distance from Sartre: I could never get used to the idea that one thinks only with one's head! The cutting voice, the voice from the head, had also cut off, dryly, the body's pulsations.

When Sartre first mentioned Freud to us, it was to speak about Stekel. At first I welcomed with extreme satisfaction the idea of bad faith, all the more since the example chosen was that of the frigid woman ... I thus killed two birds with one stone: I was learning not to believe women and, more generally, not to take at face value what others showed of themselves. The tricks of consciousness, the body's duplicity, the pretence of words would no longer hold any secrets for me. But my satisfaction was short-lived, for I soon realized that the benefit was slender. Whether women showed their pleasure or their indifference, appearances were deceptive either way. So be it. But then, what could be trusted? In girls who were attractive to me I used to look in vain for signs that could unquestionably attest to their feelings. But I had no sooner found one such sign than another one came along to contradict it. Of course this exaggerated attention to a look, an intonation, would quickly make my company less than desirable. I came to think that, with women at least, it was best to take things as they occurred without questioning feelings: the language of love was far too uncertain. Still, detecting the bad faith of others wasn't

too hard. At least I could attribute to myself an
uncommon perspicacity. But when it came to oneself,
how could one recognize it operating, this awful bad
faith? Did one have to spy on oneself non-stop, place
oneself under auto-surveillance, so as to be sure that
one wasn't at it again? But at what point did one slide
from true to deceptive emotion, from a clear gesture to
borrowed behaviour? Nothing any longer was proof
against the suspicion of fraud. Was there, then, no way
of being just simply natural? But Sartre would have
easily demonstrated to us that there was nothing more
fake than wanting to be natural, than declaring oneself
natural. For me there was no way out. From being an
ideal, lucidity became a prison. Transparency was
nothing but a snare.

I suspected that language had something to do with
this disillusionment. Certainly, it was the same
misfortune that had befallen both of us, language and
me! If the word couldn't coincide with the thing, how
could I ever have coincided with myself? The
fraudulent language that forced us to *declare* ourselves
was at the origin of this bad faith, into which each of
us, in good faith, was at every moment in danger of
sliding. It was pure madness to try to join what had
been sundered once and for all.

No doubt a remedy was possible, one I thought to
find in what Sartre offered as the years went by. His
capacity to express himself in all the genres of the
written – all the while accepting the 'rules of the genre'
and even going one better than them as if to lay bare
their arbitrariness – this polymorphism staggered me. It
was like a game, it was like a challenge! Now, what if I

wrote a play, something to put metaphysics on the stage
of a boulevard theatre! What if I wrote a script, or a
novel, or a pamphlet! Or a big work of philosophy
constructed as a serial! For Sartre, no sooner said than
done. For me, so many stray impulses or endeavours
which came to nothing. But I have always retained
something of this urge towards multiple expression: I
don't believe in a hierarchy of forms, any more than in
one of pleasures. What does the cask matter, provided
one gets drunk ... This playful aspect of Sartre, this
sprightly vigour of a demiurge who was still a kid, was
so obvious to me that it led to a misunderstanding. One
day in Spring 1944 Sartre told me of his intention to
start (I must have heard 'to produce') a review once the
war was over: he asked me to collaborate on it. 'With
pleasure,' I said. 'There's a job that appeals to me
particularly: I would like to be a "boy", you know the
ones who do dance-steps round the star.' I had
immediately associated with the word *revue* not
Gallimard but the Casino de Paris. For my part, my
blunder repeated the blotting-paper incident at the H
school: to do a few smooth dance-steps, to sing a light
popular song, wonderful, but to have to fill pages with
writing, no thank you. Perhaps, also, afraid not to be
Sartre's son or his uniquely chosen one, I wished to
turn him into Mistinguett and take my modest place in
his troupe of boys, where I had some chance of being
his favourite ... But, if we admit that a misunderstanding also says something about whoever provokes it (I
doubt if it could have happened with the excellent
Monsieur Charlier), the fact is that Sartre as a person,
at least in my eyes, was incompatible with nothing, at

any rate not with Music Hall; the fact is that there were
in him the resources of an actor capable of playing all
the parts – which made him very far from being a ham,
very far from being a literary hack, and which turned
him later into someone fascinated by the personalities
of actors. Question: what did Sartre *believe* in?

But, among Sartre's words, it wasn't precisely those
that could claim to be concepts, like bad faith, or
contingency, nor the 'in-itself for-itself' which gave us
such a headache, we poor little for-itselves so deprived
of any in-itselves, no it wasn't those that I considered
belonged to his basic language, it wasn't those that
silently impregnated me. I was secretly partial to
others, ones he used bizarrely, and whose strangeness I
was keen to maintain (I wouldn't have liked to have to
write an essay on them). Obscene, for instance.

At eighteen one isn't too concerned about not being
consistent. Later, more so. At the very least one tries to
explain one's disarray. *La Nausée* and *Nadja* could
therefore captivate me equally and at the same time, a
bit in the same way as when a few years before, totally
lost in my reading, I'd been able to go in one stride
from *Rocambole* to *Le Grand Meaulnes*. In me the
overcoming of the imaginary and the exaltation of the
marvellous got on well together. Besides, I didn't see
any major contradiction between Sartre's sinister
Bouville and Breton's fantastic Paris. I certainly
needed not to see any, needed the principle of
communicating vessels between the real and the surreal
not to be confuted.

4 London in Venice

Gale, the lull recalls or foretells it, arcs in the sky that rend as much as they join, storms, explosions, shipwrecks, no stable line, no definite shape, no assured distinctions, the fall of a sun that could be rising or setting, whirlwinds of stuff and colours, fires and avalanches of unknown provenance, the elements both fused and confused, this whole expanse of water is a cracked stone and this wall is all haze, raging weather, is it the end or birth of a world? No longer any regulating principle and yet this isn't a blind, furious destruction, rather harmony found at last, nothing left but light, the fulfilled promise of a transformation.

Man is absent. Not dead but erased. Neither watched nor watching, even if he still regards as a spectacle, as his own creation, this world making and unmaking and reconstructing itself without him. Here is this man already in the state of something left-over, of a ruin, almost dissolved in the invisible, like that edifice blurring among the browns, like that abandoned ship, like that reflection of mist.

At this moment, Turner is for me the whole of painting and painting the whole of reality.

I come out of the Tate Gallery, I walk along the Thames and I am in Venice, later I have a rendezvous with Pearl. Disoriented, floating in the damp air, I look for a bus-stop, the vaporetto station, to find a line, a route, to go towards a centre that should be there. The December rain is cold, the town is by the sea, there is wind and swirl on the lagoon, on the river. Pearl and I shall look for shelter.

Painting takes possession of me without warning, in a sudden vertigo, in successive waves coming from further and further away. But I don't stay in it long. Words get the better of me and, with words, the distribution of time, of tasks, of meaning, which tear me away from the violence of painting – or its serenity, for in painting I find the alliance of opposites. Having fallen out of love with the eloquence of pure sensibility, I move away from its beauty which for me resides perhaps in this: that, with the same gesture and in the same finite place, a painter can both call forth and exorcize chaos. By making it visible, he necessarily orders it. When I've received this terror and this certainty from painting, I can then go about my business, with a more troubled soul but a surer step. I've recognized, because of having approached it, because of having momentarily yielded to its spell, that in a place apart there exists another space. To verify that it exists is enough for me. I can then go back to the usualness of days, of others and of myself: I can trust words again as if I had newly recovered the assurance, at least for a while, until the next nocturnal light, that words come from that space, that it isn't language that makes language. Sometimes the everyday – repeated, discontinuous – seems to me to be only a gap between two painted canvasses, between two forgotten dreams.

The space of the dream and of the painting: I find
the same powers in both, in each I drink at the same
reliable source. They call to one another. They
reinforce my conviction that words translate askew.
They lead me to believe that language can only say
what is already accomplished, that it arrives late, to
move in like an abusive proprietor, an arrogant master,
once the work has been done – the work of the obscure.
No assemblage of words, not even the most mineral of
poems, will ever make me a witness of the emergence!

Above all not to talk about painting. Above all not to
tell one's dreams. To write, when it's possible, *from*
painting and to return from dreams as one returns from
the ends of the earth. I fear insomnia, that ruthless
naked lucidity, more than nightmares. Insomnia, or the
real become nightmare, the relentless inexorable attack
of the inanimate. Sometimes, when I've taken part for
too long in the endless production, the great consump-
tion of words and my voice comes from my head, when
I've lost all contact with what there is *before*, I think of
myself as a daytime insomniac. Then there is only one
god: Hypnos; only one remedy: to abandon myself to
his flow, to his rhythm. In the morning, borne by him, I
might have recovered my voice. I think anyone who
considers that time spent sleeping is dead time is
someone condemned to death. Sleep is my source.

I have forgotten the name of the pub where Pearl
and I are to meet. Yet I'm sure that I'll rejoin her since
I haven't lost her, since I caught a glimpse of her in
one of those watercolours by Turner that I'm still
impregnated by, or else it's because I've dreamt of her
so many nights. She doesn't speak French. I've only got

my lycée English, and Chaucer or Hume will be of
little use ... Is it this disability which, at this moment,
makes me lose my bearings in this foreign city? Yet I'm
feeling happy to be alive, in this state of confident
anticipation that is mine. I can already see us rushing
headlong towards each other. Her hair will be wet.
Between the long brown strands I shall see the two
small lakes of her light eyes. And I can anticipate
everything to follow. It's going to happen, I'm sure of it,
but like so many brief miracles: the scalding tea, the
black taxi, the gleaming brick house, my greeting Mrs
Simpson the landlady (she wears an apron with purple
flowers), a wooden staircase, the thick door painted
white, the window ajar, drops of rain on the sill, Pearl
naked in the narrow bed, I don't know what comes from
her, what comes from me.

I don't like what's brought about. I like what comes.

One evening, many years ago, I met Roland at the
house of some friends. About to leave France, probably
for a long time, he was storing a few canvasses there.
One of them lay on the floor, in a corner of the room
where we were having supper. As Roland felt a bit
down, the conversation was quite brisk, with the help of
the wine, so as to silence the unease of impending
separation. My gaze was drawn to the canvas, briefly at
first then more and more often. I could hear the
laughter, I was taking part in what was being said but,
in the hollow of this unforeseeable movement that
makes a conversation playful, an impulse was becoming
flesh, a fixed idea was insinuating itself: *I want it*. A
few hours later, I was walking up the Boulevard

Saint-Germain, hiding the canvas under my raincoat. I
had paid Roland the price he was asking, he had said
the usual things: how pleased he was that I had liked
his painting, etc. And yet, I was fleeing like a thief.

Even today, I can't remember that evening without
feeling disturbed, I can only look at that painting, now
hanging on the wall in my office, surreptitiously. I have
other paintings at home. I forget some for months; into
one of them I plunge every day, into its blue space.
With Roland's painting it's different, I shall never
know how to use it. But very quickly I knew why I'd
had to appropriate it on the spot. It's because I
recognized it, because I found represented in it what
I'd already seen elsewhere but which I myself wouldn't
have been able to hold in an image. It's as if I'd told
Roland, on emerging from a dream – but from a dream
which would itself have been the reflection of a
memory and that memory would itself have been the
screen on which was projected a previous memory, and
so on to infinity – yes, it's as if I'd attempted to tell
Roland, this man I hardly knew: there is water and
marble, the surface of the water is quite flat, without a
ripple, there is marble, marble steps lead to the
expanse of grey water, it looks like a piazzetta in
Venice encircled by palazzi but it's not Venice, it's like
an arm of the sea which penetrates a town, yet there's
no current, it's more like a dead arm, there's also an
industrial plant there, industrial chimneys, I think,
something metallic – not a plant, a factory rather, a
disused factory, so it's like two kinds of buildings, two
architectures, both from another time, both no longer in
use, next to one another, they don't merge, their being

together in one image is unusual, they co-exist, that's all, ignoring each other, together only for the person who looks at the painting. And Roland, as dictated to by me, punctuated by 'likes', 'roughlys', 'it was like that without being that', a dictation painful as any transcription of what one believes to be extremely precise since one saw it more intensely than one will ever see anything in the pale light of day – Roland had fixed the thing, without omitting a detail, taking into account my successive corrections, anxious to represent it as I wanted it to be. He'd only added one detail which wasn't my invention, showing in a corner of his painting a small seated figure. That figure alone was blurred, awkwardly drawn. Simultaneously near and far, the figure looks at the painting in which he appears, as if he were giving the painting to the spectator and were destitute of everything but gaze: the figure observes the scene but the scene doesn't belong to him. The factory, the expanse of water, those deserted buildings do without him. Venice, in its endless morning after, Venice already absent to Venice, has no need of the figure's absence or of his presence. The figure knows it, *he* is the inanimate one, more than matter, more than the thing painted, more than the dead water and the cold marble.

The page I've just written took it out of me. I had to search for words, they resisted coming and I resisted them as soon as I'd adopted them. Now that they are written and leave me as unsatisfied as the mute young man in the painting, I'm listening to them. What primal scene did I intend both to evoke and to annul there, in that enigmatic combination of empty architectures?

The fascination remains, and the sudden emotion I felt in front of that canvas and my gaze drawn to it as to a magnet and the urgent need I had to take possession of it and bring it home and that bizarre feeling of having stolen it and of needing to hide it from the passers-by who couldn't care less – I'm keen to preserve all that. I shall not allow words to release me from my image. Why should meaning be stronger than image to designate what no meaning encompasses?

I walk along the docks in London and the small streets of Venice, I go towards Hyde Park and the Salute. Pearl's slight body will be my square and piazzetta, my water and palace. She's waiting for me, she's there under the pub's red and black signboard on which, through my misty glasses, I make out the blurred letters of a word whose meaning – God is on my side! – I don't know. The mouths of two strangers merge under the sign where words fail.

From where does the love of beginnings come to us if not from the beginning of love? From the love which will have no future and perhaps in that way no end.

How soft and urgent her voice is! In the exchange of a breath, in a yes that acquiesces – to what? to the sharing of ecstasy? – these two young people who can be only strangers to each other are fused for a night. They fall asleep to old Turner blessing them and wake up to Mrs Simpson's bubbling teapot while outside the rain hasn't stopped.

5 Death of summer

The long holidays started right after prize-giving. No interval or gap. Nature – bourgeois nature – abhors a vacuum. The black car took us to the big house in Cabourg where another order awaited us, a schedule of pleasures as rigorous as the H school's ritual or, later, the lycée's time-table (or, today, the sequence of analytic sessions ...). Could it be then that the unpredictable, if it arises, only appears within a fixed frame, the unusual only in the thick of repetition?

The first morning, we would find our rusty spades and our seaside buckets under the hedge where we had faithfully forgotten them the previous year; in the afternoon, our bicycles in the garage; and, the last days, when September came, my mother would take out of a trunk the big red woollens smelling of camphor, which heralded our return to Paris. Equinox and return to school, high tides and new exercise-books, it was one and the same thing. In this sense, my family had perfectly succeeded with my education: I saw no difference between the order of things and the social order. A single grammar governed us. A *sou* is a *sou* but *chou* in the plural becomes *choux*, a servant serves at table but it's Grandfather who carves the roast, children go to bed before grown-ups but get up earlier,

rivers flow into the sea, the road goes from the Rue de
Courcelles to Cabourg and from Cabourg to the Rue de
Courcelles, one dries oneself after swimming or one
catches a cold, an error of taste is the same as a
spelling mistake, a rude word could well be a mortal
sin and bad thoughts criminal acts. I would thus have
been able to line up in a disordered way everything
that made up my order, unable to decide whether these
were elementary statements or inflexible command-
ments. In any case, their legitimacy was equal, and,
should any one of these propositions have been
doubted in my presence, I would have felt as dizzy as if
an unbeliever had said to my face that God didn't exist.
No, I would have been even more disturbed for, in
such a well-organized and stable world, a world so
much in control of its time and space, what need was
there to appeal to God?

Between arrival and departure then, a strict arrangement of games, an immutable organization of the days –
beach in the morning; garden in the afternoon – a
perfectly organized 'social life' of which my brother, as
far as the children were concerned, was the Lord
Chamberlain: games of croquet and tennis matches,
sack and spoon races, ping-pong balls and shrimping
nets, he had the knack of regulating the sequence of
our activities without controlling them. Every Thursday
– never any other day – we would invite some friends
and, on the second Thursday in August – never the
third – it was the 'big tea' which would be attended by
the children of the neighbourhood, whom we sometimes
hardly knew. That day there would be a profusion of
flans and apricot tarts, of custard and fresh lemonade.

Our prestige was then at its height. Were we aping the
adults or were the adults aping us? It was a bit as in
the stories of the Comtesse de Ségur: the two worlds,
that of the adults and that of the children, mirror each
other so faithfully that there's no way of saying which is
the reflection. Certainly, our uncle seemed to favour
horse-racing over sack-racing and bridge over ping-
pong, but where was the difference? No doubt, as one
grew corpulent, one had to change one's playground.
And then we would all meet in the dining-room,
wearing, in short trousers or long, the same white
flannel and laughing politely at the same joke uttered
by our grandfather: 'Today we're having *faux-filet*
[sirloin]. But being *false* won't make it any less good.'
Believing oneself a Guermantes born, how quickly one
reverts to the level of the Verdurin!

Was I happy during these summers that were
repeated almost without variation for nearly ten years
until my grandmother's death, followed, shortly afterwards, by the sale of the house? That's a question
without an answer: a child is scarcely concerned with
happiness; he registers things, he catches them, he's
constrained to make what surrounds him his. But, even
today, the image I retain of the big house, of the
arrangement of the rooms, of the distribution of
bedrooms among its various occupants, of the garden
paths, of the flower-beds and orchard, of the slightly
rotten wooden stairs that went down to the beach, of the
basin concealed in a cupboard at the entrance in which
we had to wash our hands before meals, of the wicker
chairs on the terrace and of the small Japanese
drawing-room – this image, which is rich and

inexhaustible only for me and of which everyone has
their equivalent, remains unaltered. Since that far away
time I've had occasion to go through Cabourg, and even
once, imprudently, to take there the woman I then
loved. We went along the beach in the direction of the
house. I wanted ... what exactly? Less for her to know a
place in my memory than no doubt for me to be
reassured, through the gaze of a supposedly favourable
witness, that the insistence of my remembering, that the
intensity of the illusion were not without reason: that
my hallucination was truthful! But, when we approached, when I glimpsed from the top of the dunes
the brown-tiled roof then the white fence, I started
running, leaving my companion in the lurch, forgetting
my earlier concern to show her the house, to make her
touch the thing with her look. 'Why are you running
like that, like a madman?' the young woman shouted
after me. As to why, I had some idea. What was I
running after? I believe I shall never know.

I wasn't trying to make sure that nothing had
changed. I knew that the house had become a
rest-home for the Electricity Board's depressed staff, as
if it were their turn to be deprived of current; I was in
no way surprised that the impeccable lawn had been
overtaken by weeds, that makeshift, that is to say
miserable, buildings had been erected along its wings,
that machine-made tiles had been used to plug the hole
a shell had made in the roof; I imagined a refectory
with formica tables and metal chairs, perhaps even a
dormitory or a television room in my grandmother's
four-windowed bedroom. Nothing gets lost, nothing is
created, everything runs down: I knew the physics

lesson by heart. It wasn't disappointment, therefore,
that I experienced that day. I would certainly, on the
contrary, have felt disappointed and betrayed if the
large house had remained intact, if the geraniums had
still been in bloom in the dark-green painted urns, if
the paths, their outline now erased, had still shown
signs of a rake, if, in other hands, the *thing* had
remained the same. That's when I would have felt
dispossessed. Strangers – upstarts, my grandparents
would have said, forgetting their own social ascent –
would have acquired our delicious summers, would
have intruded into my private domain, would have
shamelessly stolen from me a part of my identity.

I understand now why it was this woman rather than
any other whom I had summoned to a rendezvous which
I knew in advance would fail, which I even hoped
would. Claire, so ill-named, had, throughout the years
that we'd more or less spent together, remained
unpredictable to me. I could only foresee one thing,
almost without respite, which was that I couldn't be
sure of anything with her or, by immediate rebound,
within myself either. There is, coming from the woman
one loves, a worse threat than that of being left one
day: that of being rejected on the spot, instantly,
cancelled by just a look which lingers one doesn't know
where and she probably doesn't know either. Suddenly,
something – it's impossible to have the faintest idea
what it is – absorbs her entirely. It would be better –
one thinks then – to be jealous of a rival than of this
overflowing absence. Claire was the uncertainty which,
from one month to the next, from one second to the
next, devastated or transfigured my present. By taking

her to the house in Cabourg, across the broad beach at
low tide that stretched from the Dives to the Orne,
along this sea that was grey whatever the weather, I
regained mastery and possession of a perfectly demar-
cated place. That it had become unrecognizable hardly
mattered to me, as I've said. On the contrary, the
modifications it had undergone through the effect of
circumstances guaranteed that it was unchangeable for
me, and for me alone. If Claire never stopped escaping
me, even when she was beside me, it was enough for
me, by contrast, to evoke the house of those summers
for it to be mine, without it being touched in any way
by the erosion of time. I could wholly hold it in
memory, I could wholly possess it in imagination. We
would never let go of each other. And furthermore, after
having lived there so long, it was right that the house
should dwell in me.

The image of closure can be that of prison or of
paradise, of naked destitution or of manna: it's all there
or nothing's there; it depends. I think I've never got
over that contradiction. For a long time I had a taste
only for travel: walking for hours, without reference-
points, in an unknown town; sleeping, making love,
each night in a hotel room with fresh linen; hearing,
like simple popular music, a language that's foreign to
you; allowing the *granita di limone* to melt slowly while
discovering a Masaccio in a dark corner of the church,
after having dropped in the box a few *lire* to turn on a
light bulb; climbing the slopes of Mount Corinth at the
hottest time of day; visiting the Amsterdam zoo and
conversing with its giraffes, when one hasn't ever set

foot in the zoo at Vincennes; taking a winding road and, after kilometres of sand and rock, finding oneself in biblical country, on the Lassithi plateau; to be nothing but gaze, thirst and fatigue, movement, pursuit, awakened and never satiated senses. But today, the more time goes by, the more my territory becomes circumscribed. One street to cross to go from my flat to the publishing house where I work in the morning, the same street to cross again to my consulting-room where I officiate in the afternoon; the newsagent is fifty metres away, the tobacconist a couple of steps. It's true that to buy a book or get a haircut I have to cross the boulevard and, to go to the cinema, push as far as Odéon, but all that would almost fit inside the boundaries of the Cabourg garden, and neither here nor there do I discover the least monotony. Beyond these frontiers I'm rarely in a festive mood. Could it be that I've become, with the passing of the years (not to write bluntly: with growing old), immensely phobic? But, on the other hand, anything that may signify the 'between-ourselves' weighs me down, everything that's said in the agreed, allusive language of a milieu or else is hidden within a family's silence irritates me: psychoanalysts quoting Freud among themselves, writers of the *Nouvelle Revue Française* remembering Paulhan or Queneau, I listen, I learn, I'm amused (in the second case), but it's back in the street that my thoughts can breathe.

The closure of the lycée. The closure of the house. The one reduplicated the other. Life in the class-room and life during the holidays were mutually ignorant of, but did not exclude, each other. They were just totally

insulated from one another: they didn't care much in
my family about my scholastic performance, and I was
never asked at the lycée where and how I had spent my
holidays; I left my lycée class-mates at the beginning of
July and met them again on the first of October, and the
Cabourg gang came together again in the first days of
summer to dissolve with the September tides. Such a
sharp separation between the two worlds might seem
hard to believe. Yet that's how it was. For me there was
nothing excessive or enigmatic in it. It suited me then
and I still consider it excellent. I see an abuse of power
in the notion that a single place could claim to contain
everything – I suspect a totalitarian annexation! At the
lycée I had the experience, fortunately short-lived, of
'organized leisure'. What business was it of theirs?
Were they going to teach us hide-and-seek, would we
have to play cops and robbers under the benevolent
eyes of our teachers who, having become cops, would
consequently rob us of our pleasures? Nor would I have
appreciated my uncle, who had had dealings with the
Jesuits, giving me advice on my Latin translations. The
Gaffiot dictionary on the one hand, croquet on the
other. I certainly didn't want any teacher-parent or
parent-teacher. I found my freedom in the absolute
respect accorded to this division of power, in this strict
demarcation of spaces. In Freud's metapsychology, it
was the 'topographical' perspective that was from the
start more immediately accessible to me: several
locations are necessary in oneself to preserve any
possibility of being oneself.

In fact, the Pasteur patch of ground and the Cabourg
patch were less different than I thought. The distance

between them made their similarity easier to deal with: there's no danger of confusing two doubles if they live in different continents, apart. But swimming and lessons, homework and games in the garden, were subject to rules that were equally precise and obvious enough not to have to be spelled out. A game without rules would have terrified me as much as an essay without a subject, as compulsory free drawing or that postcard I had to write every summer to Aunt Geneviève, even though she was considered to be fanciful: 'Well, tell her whatever you want, it doesn't matter what.' The basic rule of psychoanalysis which stipulates that one say 'everything that comes to mind' would certainly not have suited me.

In the winter season, as in the summer period, our employments were discreetly policed. Both societies in which I had my assigned place excluded any event, even the slightest one, which by virtue of being external to them would have done them violence. Events could only occur in their bosom, inside the system. The Pasteur system and the Cabourg system had even allowed for the circumstances when such events could happen and, so as better to exorcize them, celebrated them according to an unchangeable ritual, with an implacable gentleness. The event would be, for instance, at the lycée, the announcement made by the headmaster, the puppet president of our republic, accompanied by the assistant head, his prime minister, of the results of the written work. It would be, in Cabourg, the evolution of the great tea watched over by our slightly haughty grandmother, a lace shawl on her shoulders, a black band round her neck. Besides, grandmother was our bishop, and our headmaster was the 'spitting image' of Albert Lebrun, as our grandmother would have said, she who would have wanted neither the president nor the headmaster as butler: 'He has a good appearance, his references are excellent, but he is far too stupid.' I can hear her suave and regal voice from here, and she hasn't been around for half a century.

The analogy between the two systems can be taken further. At the lycée, as at the house by the sea, the *langue*, the correct *langue*, resided in things, not in the words we exchanged. We didn't endow our teachers with any particular talent, with any special eloquence. We would recognize in them, or not, the ability to teach us to read Racine or to solve an equation. Admiration was not directed to them in person, but to the optics lesson which made it possible for us, so to speak, to see with our own eyes, or to the chemistry experiment which made the litmus paper change colour – in the same way that we would blush in front of our class-mates' big sisters – after holding the test-tube over the Bunsen burner. Besides, the teachers themselves, with their crumpled clothes and their ties knotted awry, knew that they were only the humble servants of Knowledge, the zealous menials of Literature, passing us the dishes that others – great writers, great scholars, emperors and monarchs – had prepared in their splendid solitude, near a stove or on the battlefields.

And, in Cabourg, the conversation was lack-lustre. Even as a child, I perceived the gap between the poverty of the exchanges at table and the magnificence

of the bouquets of dahlias. Yes, elegance and refinement were there, in the upkeep of the garden, the
greenhouse in the kitchen garden, the hot peppered
prawns served on the pink-tiled terrace before lunch,
with port in a crystal decanter. Were these people
ignorant of the wealth and power of words because their
wealth, their power were all contained in their
possessions? And had our teachers dedicated themselves to what wasn't yet called Culture, because their
only possession was a diploma which gave them the
right to spend their whole life in school?

One day, I saw our history teacher run for a bus. I
was disturbed by that: what, Monsieur Jourcin, a
familiar of the *agora* and of Schönbrunn, who'd known
exile in St Helena and conquered the Arabs in Poitiers!
The conductor was helping him onto the bus: there he
was, running like us – just a bit more out of breath.
Another day, Monsieur Laurent invited me to his home,
I no longer know why. He introduced me to his
'spouse', an affable person, a bit fat, who smelled of
cooking. And there was M. Laurent, who (the day
before) had read us *Les Amours* by Ronsard, confiding
in me his prognosis for the forthcoming Tour de France.
The world was upside down. I went home as
disconcerted as if I had caught my grandparents,
during the summer, fornicating on the grass.

Thus a mere nothing would have been enough to
disrupt the beautiful arrangement of the world. How
precarious therefore was the law which I had so much
pleasure submitting to! If everyone be no longer exactly
in their place, if the flowers emigrate from their beds, if
the teachers leave their rostrum, here am I beginning to

vacillate, no longer to know where I am. So it was *I*
who required that order, that repetition, those con-
straints! Of course, I didn't formulate this discovery in
these terms at the time. And, when I had an inkling of
it, I did my best to erase it. Yet there were a few snags,
a few anomalies that disturbed me, that gave me the
fleeting feeling of a kind of discontent within my
civilization ... Brief moments escaping from the time-
table, which I didn't know what to do with: hollow
times without work and without games, without friends
and without books, when I wandered around in a mood
of desolate vacancy. And then accidents. I'm not
talking about scratches and bumps that conferred on
the everyday a bit of adventure and that could be
patched up with ointment and disinfectant, but about
fractures and wounds, about that which nastily tears
and breaks the body. I couldn't accept – and in fact I
still can't – that it's in moments of intense pleasure, of
happy exaltation, of complete harmony, that accidents
occur. A deep gash in the forehead when I jauntily
climb a wall, a fall from my bicycle which breaks my
arm when I'm going down the hill first in the race; it
seemed to me that plaster-casts and stitches existed to
penalize too much confidence. Bad marks and re-
proaches could vex me, nothing more. But this was
really too unfair! I rebelled against the idea of bowing
to this lesson of elementary science, which taught me,
brutally and without words, that one was wrong to
speak of stupid accidents, that on the contrary they
occur to put an end to an unforgivable stupidity and
make it obvious. The least excess, in our world where
everything is tamed, starting with Nature, deserves

punishment.

This mere nothing that I said earlier would be enough to make the order of our world collapse, I learned to call by its name. It was death.

I don't know if my childhood was marked by death more than other people's. I only know that in what remains of it today, in the by-now-stable image I make of it, it appears to me as if punctuated, and over a short span of time, by deaths. After my father's, which made that hollow in me where I found my shelter, one death followed another. Not a year without a funeral service; not a year without a black armband, no sooner had I put it away than I had to take it out again from the bottom of a drawer. Curiously, my family gave the event all its due and at the same time saw to it that it was hushed up. Like wealth, death needed to have its external signs: mourning clothes, then half-mourning going from black to grey and a touch of mauve for the women, Sunday morning visits to the cemetery with upkeep of the tombstone, the gift of a cruise to Spitzbergen where the midnight sun was supposed to chase away the shadow of melancholy – and that strange, so-called 'end-of-year' ceremony, which I confused with a brand of liquorice* and which, just when we had succeeded in forgetting the deceased, made us ashamed of our indifference. That day tears rose again in our eyes and prayers rose to heaven. In the same way that the finely laid-out garden at Cabourg made the trees and plants into ever-smiling servants, that the sovereign grace of my grandmother forever

---

* 'Boud'zan': whence *bout de zan*, almost *bout de l'an* (= end of year).

transformed Marie Buge into cook and Joseph Langlois into gardener, that the sea had been created for bathing and knew nothing of storm – and our conversations knew nothing of raised voices – so were these rites of mourning designed to tame death. Each time we had to appear to be sadder than the time before; my mother above all, 'the poor Fernande', was much to be commiserated with, 'alone with her two children and herself now an orphan', but it would have been unbecoming to cry out in pain and to sink into grief. Death was as natural, no – as social, as registered, as an end of season. The following summer we would find our spades again, just a bit more rusty, under the prickly hedge. Since nothing from outside must reach us, how could we have recognized death as the affront, the unforgivable assault that it is?

Hence I came to have the idea that there was no other real relationship with death than an intimate, constant, silent one. This certainty must have been established quite early when, at the age of nine, I lost my father. While the adults, in the hours and days that followed, bustled about in my presence, it happened on two or three occasions that they interrupted their conventicles, only immediately to return to them after a 'Don't worry, he's too young to understand'. At that moment I knew, without the slightest doubt, that I was the only one who 'understood'; I wished, secretly, to be the only one to live that death. They were already concerned with the consequences, with what was to become of my mother, of the too large and too expensive apartment we would have to leave; they spoke of debts to soak up or *sponge*, which seemed odd to me, for I

then couldn't 'understand' how a sponge could be put to
that use. Thus my father could be calmly disposed of as
soon as there was no longer any reason to reckon with
him, when his slightly mocking, short-sighted gaze, his
fits of anger and his laughter were no longer in season.
If, after so many years, these words 'too young to
understand' haven't been erased, it's because I refused,
during those days, to erase my father, to hold as
negligible, as null, as abstract what had only stopped
being audible and visible.

At that time I wasn't far from transposing life and
death. Since life was so fragile – my father had died
without any warning, from the consequences of acute
appendicitis – there was certainly something infinitely
less fragile than life: the bond with the person I had
lost and, later, the bond with absence, with what
doesn't directly occupy the field of vision. Suddenly, all
human beings appeared as survivors. I couldn't help
detecting in their semblance of life, in the stubbornness
applied to filling their days, in their constant worry, so
many traits of the death which, unbeknown to them,
possessed them already. Yes, death exerted its corro-
sive action on their existence, it was stealthily in them,
whereas they believed that it was ahead of them, but
always deferred. And, conversely, everything that I
could evoke as I pleased, everything that was imagined
and not present, gained in my eyes a kind of eternity. I
learned, years later, to make this imperceptible transformation effective, in the present – even to have
recourse to it as a method. The flatness of everyday life
immediately became transfigured by it. It was enough,
for instance, for me to imagine being in the métro,

when I was actually in it, for the names of the stations
to be subject to the fate of Combray or Jerimadeth, for
the haggard faces of the people opposite me to turn into
so many Flemish portraits, for there to be a parallel
between the journey to Jussieu from Porte de Champer-
ret and descending the Amazon in a kayak. One
morning, at the café, I confided the effectiveness of my
method to Sartre, naively but still a bit anxiously. I
would go so far as to see in it, I resolutely affirmed, the
only acceptable rule of life. He sniggered: 'Ah! salvation through art!', then added, thoughtfully: 'I believed
in that too. But it doesn't work.' I attempted, in my
defence, to prove to him that it was a kind of *epoché*
(Sartre had just talked to us about Husserl ...), of a
putting-into-brackets which, far from keeping reality at
a distance, gave back to reality, at last, its weight of
truth, gave it that solidity it so sadly lacked. Through
the image, I reached the essence! And there was no
reason to limit the aesthetic attitude to the contempla-
tion of works of art. But Sartre was uncompromising.
He made me ashamed of the confusion I wanted to
maintain between the imaginary and the real; all that
was old hat and, as far as that went, the surrealists had
done it better. And he slyly added: 'You should read
René Boylesve or Estaunié, they're right up your
street.' My mint soda had never tasted so bitter. The
transfiguration no longer worked. That evening, I
re-read *La Nausée*, it was great, and I admired Sartre
because he was, also, a writer. How was I to see my
way out of this? I thought I had a rejoinder: I would
renounce eternal salvation and would keep the art of
the everyday. It would be my way, modest and known

only to me, not to get bogged down in reality. As a bonus, I wasn't displeased to catch Sartre, in his turn, in the trap of bad faith. For, after all, he too must believe in the magic of words, therefore in the power of the image without which words would have no effect, to be writing six hours a day.

One morning, in Cabourg, I didn't find Blackie as usual stretched out on the red eiderdown, at the foot of my bed. I called him, I looked for him all morning. I was told that he must have gone for a walk, that these things happened to dogs, that he would certainly come back in the evening, exhausted. That evening he wasn't there, nor the next day. For several days, accompanied by Joseph Langlois, I covered miles of dunes in all directions, we went down each path of the neighbouring wood, until Joseph, who had bravely fought in the Great War, decided to report him lost. It wasn't until the following summer that my mother, inadvertently, told me at a crossroads: 'Well, that's where they found your dog run over.' So, they had wanted to spare me. I was touched by the concern and at the same time surprised. For me, who had seen my father die in his hospital bed, who was reminded by the weekly visit to the cemetery that he was stowed in a box under the earth till the end of time ('plot held in perpetuity', these strange words were carved on a corner of the tomb), why had they all done their best to hide from me Blackie's death? Perhaps only human beings had the right to die. Plants withered, animals, dogs must disappear like clouds, at the end of the morning. Unless, quite simply, my mother thought – and I always remained grateful to her for her consideration as well as for her clumsiness – that, having already been left by my father, I didn't need to be left by Blackie whom I loved, as one loves dogs, because he wouldn't leave me, because he would refuse even to run ten metres without me, except on that fatal morning when I slept longer than was my wont and some distant barking must have attracted him.

And then, I remember, that same summer my mother was watching her own mother slowly die. That death I couldn't not know about. My grandmother, after years of treatments and operations, of stays in clinics and rest-homes, had asked to spend the summer at the house. She no longer left her room, whose windows for her no longer opened on to the sea. We, the children – my brother, my cousins – didn't see her. One day, carelessly, I came across her in a corridor. 'What are you doing here?' I felt ashamed, and compassionate more than afraid: she looked, she who had been so beautiful, so haughty – our bishop with the clear, light eyes – like the old vegetable-seller in the market whom we called the witch. A professor – a 'leading medical consultant', our grandfather told us – came from Paris. He stayed for lunch, then went off. The next day, Grandmother died. I burst into sobs, and yet I hadn't liked her much: I found her cold – unaware, with the egotism of children, that it was her extreme tiredness and pain which made her keep us at a distance.

That day, the house died too. My uncle and aunt really tried, the following summers, to keep it alive, but it was no longer the same. They had their friends to stay and, when I came for a few days, I felt like a guest.

Marie the cook had left, with her custards that were my delight, and so had Joseph the gardener, with his geranium cuttings that made the modalities of reproduction even more mysterious for me. Weeds were spreading over the paths, apples rotted in the orchard, conversations, in losing their futility, also lost their innocence. One day I heard Mussolini's merits being praised, 'a real statesman', and yet, I was convinced, my grandmother wouldn't even have received him in her kitchen. That praise strongly displeased me: all my admiration was for the Negus, whom I'd seen, the previous summer when my mother had sent me to England, waving to passers-by from his hotel window. What brilliance he would have brought to our great teas, this King of Kings who wasn't much taller than me!

I went to the house for the last time in September 1939. I had fought the Great War with my father, mostly after his death, in imagination, out of love. The one that was beginning seemed to me, by contrast, stripped of all value, of anything tragic: a parody. A phoney war, I might have said, even before it came to be called that. No doubt I didn't want anyone other than my father and his companions to be able to show any courage. No one after him had the right to be mentioned in dispatches!

During that final, brief stay, a death was announced on the radio. 'One bastard less', exclaimed my aunt with a nasty smile. Thus was greeted, in the declining house, the death of ... Freud. A name I had never before heard pronounced. Yet the snappy coarseness of this funeral oration didn't appeal to me in the slightest.

Was that, in the final reckoning, what the refinements
of Cabourg hid: fear and hatred? I left the house
without regrets and even with a feeling of release, of
slight elation. At fifteen, one has only one wish: to be
without a family.

'How do *langues* die?' That's the title of an article in a
journal lying on my table. It matters little to me that the
answers given are disappointingly cautious. The title
immediately echoes back to me the end of Cabourg. For
it wasn't just a place that was escaping me, nor
childhood that was drawing to a close with its games of
croquet and its rusty spades, it was indeed a *langue*
that was ceasing to be spoken, less through lack of
speakers than through its own exhaustion. Cabourg was
quick to lose its charms – its smell of summer, its
eloquence of a bygone age – but only to pass the better
into the imaginary, another name for memory, where it
would preserve the shape I intended for it.

6 Hollows

C hildhood amnesia: I cannot share this Freudian article of faith. How is it to be understood? As the child deprived of memory, or as the adult visiting amnesia on the child? For me amnesia is characteristic of adulthood, and childhood, for ever, is our only memory. After childhood, chronology moves in with its markers, but memory is cold: that year we moved, we passed an exam, we did our military service, we got married, we were in New York, we had a book published, we fell out with a friend, Françoise was born, I stopped teaching, I broke up with Claire, no, it was she who left me, I met Claude, when was it then ... in 70? In 73? I keep my diaries of past years in a shoe-box. Why? I never look at them. Besides, what would I discover? My daily appointments, some titles of films, the name of a restaurant, of a town, of an author to read, the time of a train, a plumber's address. Hard to admit that all this mirrors a life. In the age of childhood, there are no notebooks, no dates, nothing that might make one think: I mustn't forget that, nor anything that might make one say: I shall never forget it. And yet, precisely because there's no appeal to memory, because we're not required to remember anything whatever, because there's no slot in us in which to file our archives, no concern to differentiate

the essential from the incidental, everything can then
come to lodge in us, leaving living imprints without our
intervention. Everything, no matter what, a thousand
nothings: the smell of a room, the design of an ear or of
a wallpaper, the creaking of a floor, a very thin and
very tall man, a car speeding past, a man crying, the
cistern on a train, leeches on foreheads ... and, among
this bric-à-brac, in this attic of débris, some images
less fragmented and less enigmatic, which one tells
oneself must be more powerful: one's father taking a
shower; mother in the corridor, her bathrobe half open;
father again, moaning: 'I'm done for' when the
ambulance arrives. The inventory seems infinite at first,
and then later these bits form a close weave, lines and
figures appear, the 'I remember' seems to have an
orientation, to be leaving always from the same remote
point and going always in the same direction, so that
we believe it is going to rejoin a centre. Yet the 'I' is
undoubtedly out of place here. Everyone can say,
without abusing his prerogatives too much: 'I do', 'I
think', 'I believe', perhaps: 'I dreamt'; but 'I'm
dreaming' is only uttered at the moment when the
dream is about to end. What if 'I' were absent from
memory, as from the dream, and yet, like the dream,
were taking us without our knowing and, like the dream
again, revealing to us what we are made of? It's not
their precedence in time that gives our childhood
images this aura of something eternally alive – a
brightness that doesn't tarnish or a wound that never
heals; it's that they pertain to a state, no longer
recoverable except in fleeting moments, when we were
receptive to everything around us. And we could be

receptive like that because we weren't then truly constituted: having the status of a State that wouldn't yet have established its frontiers. These will be imposed gradually through successive refusals and after various modifications of their design. In my private dictionary, childhood and memory are synonymous.

How is a field of memory formed? It needs frontiers, milestones, seasons. (Cabourg and the lycée gave me that, and there were other places.) Otherwise, days flood in, each erasing the previous one, faces are interchangeable, pieces of information follow and cancel one another. It's only in a defined space that there is room for an event, only in a continuum that beginnings may come into view and ruptures occur. Even a nomad carries his tent, a tramp has his *quartier*.

The defeat of June 1940 found us already defeated. Everything that had held me, for good or ill, held no longer. It was as if, living before the Revolution and not foreseeing it, I could nevertheless have called my time 'Ancien Régime'. I only saw the arbitrary nature, the flaws and precariousness of my kingdoms. I felt myself to be on the edge of a world itself on the edge, and all by myself a Third Estate which knew it was nothing without the means for wishing to be everything!

Shall I confess? The exodus was for us like a trip to the country. In our brand-new car we left Caen, where my brother was studying without enthusiasm (his enthusiasm took him elsewhere), two or three days before the Germans forced their way in. My brother, rediscovering all the organizational talent he had brought to our childhood games, seized the opportunity

to lead us through areas we didn't know, down small
deserted roads – no tanks or convoys – where we met
only the summer, its light, its silence. However much
my mother objected that the circumstances were hardly
suitable for tourism, my brother, very fortunately, didn't
give in and that's how we heard about the ceasefire, in
the shade of the terrace of a small café; we had just
tasted, to the slow rhythm of a trip in a flat-bottomed
boat, the sweetness and peace of the Poitou marshland.
It was, I believe, the last manifestation of our art of
living!

That manifestation, in its unawareness, didn't lack
charm, and I think of it still today, more amused than
indignant, as of a good trick played on History. But
even so: how could I have thought for so long that my
family's way of life was only a copy, more beautifully
coloured, of the order of things, and that its privileges
were only due to some divine favour? How could I have
confused the garden at Cabourg with the garden of
Eden? And how, really, could I have imagined finding
in the class-room the embodiment of a logical order
grounded in reason and guaranteeing my pleasures?

I didn't have to break violently with all that. It was
enough for me to move away from it as from an
insalubrious place of confinement, as from a sick-room.
When, at the medical examination in the lycée, I had to
blow into a machine to measure the capacity of my
lungs, the result wasn't too impressive. For the feeble
development of my rib-cage I would willingly blame the
rarefied air I had had to breathe in self-defence. No
question of inhaling that air deeply!

But where could one find something different? I

hadn't the slightest idea, therefore anything would do: the football club and the temptation to go into retreat at Solesmes, bicycle rides and games of poker, dreaming of crazy things with delicious women and searching for wisdom in Montaigne, visiting room after room of the Louvre the better to find the courage, at nightfall, on the Rue du Débarcadère, to let myself be boarded by a most obliging lady. Has adolescence become more pleasant to live through nowadays? I don't for all that want to darken the picture of my sixteenth year. It was afterwards that I could only see in it uncertainty and confusion, unease and disarray. And now, writing this book, an analogy comes to mind: in the *langue* spoken, year after year, at the lycée, as in the one exemplified, also year after year, in the rituals of summer, I was myself like a word, a syllable, like a sign, celebrating in my way, from my position as a silent child, the excellence of these codes. I could indeed, in flashes, wonder if my existence was confined to this unobtrusive sign and could thus, gradually, build up my intimate reservoir of words. All the same there was nothing to invent, other than a few minor variations on the syntax of tasks and days. But when these codes, the only ones I knew, began to shrink before my eyes, to dry up – organisms from which life withdraws – the only emergency-exit available was to go and learn others, a bit at the mercy of chance encounters; I could make these codes my own, they would be less alien to me than the one whose hold I had been subjected to. Otherwise there would be a relapse, silence again, this time on the part of speech in spite of itself – and no longer, as at the time of the H school, on the part of the

speaker. I had no choice but to be either polyglot or
illiterate. So I drifted, a lost soul longing for a true
langue!

This shift towards being detached without being able
to be caught or attached elsewhere, this shift that
makes me lose my moorings without giving me map and
compass in exchange, this hollow – all this I have gone
on experiencing. It's sometimes heralded by lassitude –
will one have to devote oneself to the same tasks
indefinitely, employ oneself day after day operating the
machine of which one is only a cog, go on repeating
anaemic words? – but, most often, by nothing of the
kind. On the contrary, there's a playfulness, a facility,
like too much lightness. Then, I attend to what I do
without being in it, to what I say but not from inside.

For a while I was a teacher. I liked that métier. I was,
give or take a few years, the same age as my pupils.
Was it this slight gap that made speech pleasant and
easy, allowing it to be neither authoritarian nor
mumbling? Was it some distant identification with my
illustrious predecessors – Alain, Bergson ... – those
teachers that the Republic, and their own virtue,
assigned to the provinces so that the grey-smocked sons
of schoolmasters and grocers, the youngest sons of
peasants (the eldest, tied to the land, would take over
the farm) might be initiated into rhetoric and philosophy just like well-born Parisians? The fact is that I took
the same pleasure, once my classes were over, in
buying fresh vegetables and nectarines, figs and
octopus on the big avenue opposite the Lycée Masséna
as in explaining to the youngsters from Nice, inclined to

an easy life and to not-always-innocent deals, the
rigour of the categorical imperative or the infinite ruses
of the malignant demon. Only my own malignant
demon, all the more sly as it didn't have the features of
a devil, made any imperative inaccessible to me, even a
hypothetical one. If I taught as if I were playing, it is
because teaching was for me a game whose elementary
rules I was confident of being able to transmit, as I was
of indicating the moves that, with just a touch of
cunning or talent, would guarantee success. Success,
that's to say the verbal mastery of just about anything, a
reference to what was 'concrete' – 'let's take this piece
of chalk' – always coming at the right moment to assure
us, my audience and me, that we were not dissolving
into the clouds.

I was very convincing. I was in my element.

Once, one of my pupils said to me as we were
leaving the classroom: 'Your classes are interesting, but
something bothers me.' I was waiting to be asked to
clarify a thing or two: I might have gone a bit too fast,
the previous week, over the law of the three estates or I
had taken too much pleasure, today, in elucidating the
paradox of the liar. 'Yes, what?' 'I have the feeling that
you don't believe in them.' I was cut to the quick, but
soon pulled myself together: he must be a Christian,
that boy, he needed assurances, a rule of life, a
guarantee of Truth and Love to set against the disorders
of his teens. I myself had gone through that! I suddenly
felt much older than him and his class-mates. Yet, in
my heart, I thought he was right, I still think so today.

He had, undoubtedly, touched a nerve. When later I
even gave up teaching, this nameless boy may have had

something to do with it. 'You don't believe in your
classes.' That day I went home not feeling very proud of
myself, not even feeling like a stroll through the market.
Since then, I have attempted to transform the reproach
into a reason for self-congratulation. Everything pulls
me away from belief, from adherence to a cause, to a
doctrine, to a discourse which claims to dictate rules, to
establish authority, political discourse being only the
model for the genre. I'm suspicious of a way of thinking
that, while denying that it does so, has an answer for
everything and holds its own uncertainty at bay. At the
heart of this reticence, I find the refusal to identify a
language with truth. However, like everyone, I need
what speaks for itself. What happiness when it imposes
itself, when nothing can alter it! In the gestures of love
(sometimes); in the running of a child, wherever he may
be going; in the thirst that's quenched on the spot. Is it
therefore necessary for the body to intervene, to be
there, at the beginning and end of the movement, and
does certainty fade as soon as thinking starts? Yet
fuzziness has no more hold over me than faith. Its only
appeal is that it helps to free me from the too-
well-defined, from the classified, from the tyranny of
codes.

This moment is as familiar to me today in
psychoanalysis as it used to be in teaching – this
moment when, even though always wary of belief, we
are pained by unbelief, this vacillation which gradually,
we fear, will tip us into the hole, once the rift has been
uncovered. I don't seek to protect myself from it. I
welcome it rather as a good omen. That's because, not
being ushered in by boredom, it doesn't usher in some

generalization of the 'what's the point?' kind either. I can only picture it for myself as a hollow and I locate this hollow in language itself. When language claims to be absolute master and is ignorant of what it is heir to – a succession of deaths and murders; when it fails to recognize that its apparent light is nothing but a cast shadow: then the 'hollow' is there to remind it. If language forgets the loss inherent in it, then one must lose language, abandon it to its own arrogance. When we find it again, it will no longer be speaking all alone to itself, loving the sound of its own voice, it will remember its absence, thanks to ours; perhaps language, in its turn, will have regretted our not being there.

Where does the power of words in analysis come from? From their mobility. Rarely is this power the result of a complicated construction, of the ingenuity of a hypothesis; impossible for it to be conveyed by means of erudite terms or academic explanation. But if at a certain point words fail either analysand or analyst, it is from this hollow, from this slight gradient which trips up a hitherto assured verbal activity that, through the lack of *langue*, what has been lacking can be said as well as what has given the illusion of fulfilment: for example the face of a mother under a lamp, occupied with her sewing, while not far from her we were playing dominoes. 'To speak in my own words', they say eventually, tired of so many words ingested, borrowed, and embedded in their flesh. The claim is absurd, they know it: words are a 'shared responsibility', as the regulations of co-ownership indicate. Yet this impossible wish has to come, in its own time, when time

becomes hollow, slackens and sags, that moment when
time-tables and the use of words and distribution of
space all collapse. When words fail, it is because,
without realizing it, one is about to touch a different
earth.

The clearing suddenly discovered in the hollow of a
dense suffocating forest, where silence is a threat; the
high plateau unfolding its broad surface in the hollow
of the mountains, whose silhouette then seems furiously
morbid and tense; the sea, but I need waves; blank
spaces and margins on the page, gaps in memory and
the small of a back; the Brittany sky, that mobile light
which gives the land its curves; the stupidity which
leaves you without a thought, your head hollow, and the
beauty which, through striking you dumb, turns you
into a receptacle, momentarily gives you a soul (that I
represent to myself as an ellipse, can one imagine a
square or rectangular soul?); a parenthesis; the shell of
the Campo in Siena; a garden down below; the woman I
embrace and who will only truly be filled, one
imagines, by the child she will expect; a night in the
hollow of one's dreams, a ship at its port of call, a pool
in the depths of the harbour when the bridge of the
lock rises slowly.

Hollows are the breathing of my life. As for death,
it's a hole.

7 Erasure

P age after page inside imitation-leather covers,
scribbled pages on lined paper in letters so small
that no one could make them out for certain,
they'd have to be deciphered, given a meaning they
don't succeed in conveying, they insist on nothing,
there's too much fear there, moreover they don't ask to
be read, the idea is only to lay down marks instead of
the hollowing emptiness, or instead of the brimming
plenitude, it's a question of encircling by means of
innumerable tiny lines, infinitesimal traces, claw-
marks, scratches, of encircling, exorcizing an ill of
unknown origin but whose nature is only too well-
known, an endlessly-examined ill, a diagnosis refined
each day, a never-ending series of ill-formed letters,
that is how – mirrored in the black notebook – he sees
himself, pages that don't ask to be read yet could go on
asking for ever, could go on repeating for ever, whether
one page or one hundred is all the same, it should be
only a scream, convulsive movements, an agitated body
seeking a comfortable position without ever finding one,
for there isn't such a thing for somebody in the grip of
insomnia, or else it could be a fever with its procession
of images, of innumerable passers-by crossing a vast
square, but these are words, explanations, analyses, a
punctilious effort to grasp a thread and it snaps or

doesn't lead anywhere, then another one, slightly
different, not really, a sterile refrain, he's aware of that,
an exhausting exhausted litany, a soliloquy, but a cold
not a whimpering one, the avowal of his impotence to
understand what's happening to him, he thought he'd
loved earlier on, he found women lovable, no harm had
come from them, rather sweetness, pleasure, gaiety,
sometimes a slight boredom, yes, in that respect it was
easy, he was up to it, but for a few months now, no,
more, a year, more, it doesn't matter, it's no longer like
that at all, he can no longer get hold of anything, he's
stagnating, he's wobbling, he's sucked into the sands,
the more he stirs the more stuck he is, he doesn't
understand, he repeats he doesn't understand, he's the
captive, of what? of her? of images? but these images
aren't his, they don't emanate from him, they're a
foreign body, that's it, he has a foreign body inside
him, she's his tumour, he can't extirpate it without
tearing himself to pieces, he's in love with this tumour,
he can't do without it, and he can't control its growth.

When all's going well between them, he calls that
phase remission.

He knows that she's not in control either, that she
herself is inhabited, driven, possessed by something
that she's not in possession of but that goes through
her, agitates her, pushes her to and fro, to come
towards him then stride away then disappear then
reappear, his turmoil only the effect of her turmoil,
therefore the love of turmoil and the torments of love
shouldn't be confused, therefore he doesn't love her,
that's it, that's clear. For how long? Not even till this
evening.

He exhorts himself: drop it, you're wasting your time, your life, pull yourself together, free yourself from this shadow, open the door, the windows; he makes resolutions, he confides orders to his notebook, sets himself a strict time-table, with hourly slots, limited and prosaic tasks, all equal – to tidy his books, to fill the fridge, to start an article –, during the day that's one thing, but what about the evening? In the evening, go out with Natalie, there's a delightful woman, things are simple with her, simple, do you hear, just what's needed in the way of emotion, of hope, but not this elation that already carries within it this dejection. Even a change of air would be something. Something, do you hear? Already, he no longer hears.

He reprimands himself: aren't you ashamed? He prostrates himself, he looks at himself as if from outside: you haven't done anything for days and days now, nothing, it's weeks since you've been able to take responsibility for yourself and why? Because you only answer to what emanates from her, you're magnetized, all you can do is place yourself on her trajectory: dead time, empty words, an automaton's gestures – you're nobody.

He argues: *now*, that's not you, that isn't your lot, you're an active boy (he no longer dares to say man), full of life – buoyant; *therefore*, he makes a decision: it's over. And it so happens that, without his having anything to do with it, the decision dwindles, becomes altogether cautious (what if he disappeared for a week?), that already the project has become burdened with anxiety: has he really assessed the consequences, calculated the risk? He's no fool: why a week? So that

she'll be the one to come running, to reproach him for
his absence, for his silence, for his complications, for
his awful character, so that she'll be the one to throw
herself into his arms, so that it'll begin again, begin at
last, as these things should begin, in wonder, excitement, turmoil of the soul, quivering of the body, the
slow magic of a beginning, a first time, unexpected,
expected, found or found again, one doesn't know
which. Are you raving or what? There'll no longer be a
first time. You can't force it so that what hasn't
happened will happen.

He notes, as a neutral, lucid observer: that's how it
is, the two of you don't know what ties you, what unties
you. All the letters you think you're exchanging come
back to you marked: not known at this address.

He forecasts: it can't change, destined to disappoint
each other, to be not there for each other, destined to
oscillate inside the same circle, if you get out of it it
won't be your own doing, it'll be through some event
not subject to the attraction-repulsion of your mol-
ecules! An external event.

The event is slow in coming.

He's occupied, possessed, invaded by an absence.
Yes, but he also knows that if a woman were all his, he
would have to be all hers. Then he would flee. He has
fled. She gets away. They're too much alike: what if she
were his female double? They're too unlike: should he
make sure of that? Two strangers; two others. Could he
have been totally mistaken about what can be expected
of love?

He spends his time in the black notebook demarcat-
ing this territory of absence. He desperately tries to

grasp what isn't there, in her, in him, between them. He wants to stop this endless movement that takes their bodies away from each other and brings them back together again. To keep a diary to keep *her*. His notebook is an embrace he would have the power to prolong, to bring to an end, at his inclination. His pen is a claw. He is a clerk of the court.

Against whom to institute proceedings? Whereas ... Whereas ...

Today he notes down the names of the hotels where they spent a night, a few days, he remembers the most ordinary ones, they're the ones he prefers: *Hôtel du Lion d'Or*, *Hôtel de France*, *de la Poste*, *du Centre*, it's with them, with these names joined together, that a poem, perhaps a novel, could be made, without there being any need to superimpose a word. Adding them up would give what? He draws up lists, as others do of women they've known. He names the foreign towns where they stayed and like a chant or a prayer minus God. He only wants and only finds names. Nothing but names of places, of towns, of hotels, of restaurants, of cafés. No sentences surrounding them, no commentary. Names only, his only certainties.

Or else he rediscovers itineraries, roads, often they used to drive for hours at nightfall, with short sentences, long silences, unmeasured time, a peculiar sort of space, after which he would take her home or bring her back to his place, he can't quite see the difference any longer. He unfolds maps, plans, they crossed many frontiers, tried many languages, it's when they were in an unknown town, both strangers, that they stopped being strangers to each other.

He notes that with her he knew only short-stay places.

He tries to guess where he went wrong: wanting, at all costs, to get at what she is.

He's lost the sentence. He no longer knows where the main clause is, the subordinate clause, the object, the subject. He's an indistinct being, without an outline. He looks for an elementary grammar. A handbook.

Then came the night animals. He saw them rise up with some terror. Yet they weren't monstrous beasts from the dawn of time. No: a horse racing across fields, a porpoise leaping out of the water, a bird cleaving the air towards the ground. Animals all moving, unpredictably, with a mad freedom but capable of domestication, given a bit of patience. Only the transformation was in the opposite direction, towards more wildness. Woman, that woman, would never be the gentle and faithful companion of man. And it was he who, like an idiot, followed in her footsteps, prisoner of this pitiful idiocy that made him believe that if only he found the necessary words she would love him as he wanted to be loved by her. To find the words, the word she wanted to hear, the word that would clinch it, the password. The glossary. The syntax. To become mobile again, with his own movement. To be horse, bird, porpoise.

At least night was populated, animated, full of dramas, of scenes. Worse sometimes were the days that he called white days. White* as nights can be or the page that hostilely refuses even one letter of the

* *Nuits blanches* = sleepless nights.

alphabet, or exhausted memory, or thought when nothing drives it any longer. He would go and sit in a park, anonymous old-age pensioner on his iron chair, in front of a sand-pit where children were busy with their temper-tantrums, weeping with grief over a spade, a coveted bucket, he would wait near them for time to pass and time wouldn't pass. He would sit at a table in a restaurant because the clock at the crossroads said it was lunch-time. He would devise his meal with care and forget to taste the dishes the waiter brought him. He wondered how they, all of them, managed to be nourished on the menu of their days. He envied them, felt sorry for them, no longer knew which. He would go to a cinema, then to another one. The street would sweep away the images at one fell swoop. He would read the paper line by line, including the classified ads. Nothing but the paper. He considered he was already better when a poster, a shop-sign attracted him. Then the things around were no longer so hostile, no longer utterly silent, they beckoned to him and he – he felt a little less erased in the city.

One day he stopped filling the imitation-leather notebook with these thousands of illegible signs, he no longer repeated these marks in black ink. It was like one of those mornings when, on waking up, you discover that the fever has abated. You still feel weak, tender, but the noises heard are no longer blows; voices are soft again; you long for a hot croissant: that's it, you're cured.

Of what? – He was no longer interested to know.

8 The smell of closed rooms

I t was a year or two after the end of the unchained madness of war that I had a first encounter with the madness in chains, the kind that's locked up. A couple of friends had invited me to the mental hospital of Saint-Maurice (or, as I knew it, the Charenton asylum) where they both worked as house doctors. After lunch, in the same way that one suggests a walk, they asked me if I felt like going round the ward over which they presided. 'Here, put on this white coat.' In the morning we had walked along the Marne, then hired a boat to go down the river. It was a beautiful spring day, quite warm. We were in good spirits, the women wore sandals and flowered dresses, we had our arms round their waists, I could almost see myself wearing light pantaloons, a scarf and cap, singing a love-song. But now my friend was unlocking a grey door, was saying a few words to a warder who opened another door with a grille, and I followed them, in my white coat, a little less cheerful than before and already a little ashamed of my curiosity. We were in a women's ward. A nauseating mixture of smells: of ether, bleach and the sourness of a canteen. The smell of the hawthorn in the morning immediately vanished; forgotten too was the enjoyment of the conversation in the Juvenins' small house a hundred metres beyond these walls!

I saw a female inmate come towards me from the end of a corridor, determined, preoccupied, like those solitary dogs one passes in the street; then, when she was quite close, she smiled at me. I smiled back. She came even closer until her face was almost pressing against mine. She simpered. Haggard old woman or excited young girl? No way of knowing. A comical or pathetic moment? The usual reference-points were of no help to me. I vaguely heard some words: 'Ah, the new doctor, how young and handsome he is!' I was scared, I would have preferred it a hundred times over if she'd insulted me. But this absurd display of love, coming from God knows where, addressed to God knows whom, borne by God knows what, this shrill volubility contrasting with the dark fixity of her gaze left me dumbfounded. I was mutely witnessing the affectionate and light-hearted Eros of the banks of the Marne transfigured into a demon, an incubus, a witch. Juvenin had disappeared, other patients had come out of the ward and in a circle round us were watching the scene laughing. When my friend came back he simply asked the woman: 'So how are you today, Madame Leroux?', and right away it was over between her and me. I can no longer quite remember the explanations I was given: florid hysteric, manic state, erotic delusion ... I didn't care. Much later I learnt how to read psychiatric textbooks. I don't scorn them, as it's the fashion to do nowadays, but I understood at the time of this brief visit to Charenton that, had I ever become a psychiatrist, it would have been less to face madness and measure myself against it than to protect myself from it. Locked doors, closed rooms, each builds his walls within himself.

In order to hear Lacan speak, some ten years

later, one also had to go into a hospital (but it was at
Sainte-Anne), also go through a door opened from the
inside by a female warder, also go through a women's
ward. And I sometimes reflected that *there* it wasn't
the white coats that offered a protective barrier but
the discourse. The idea was naive, certainly silly, but
it came to me all the same while I attempted to make
sense of the 'graphs' on the blackboard ('Mannoni,
would you be so kind as to wipe all that off ...') and
the suspicion never quite left me: on the other side
of the amphitheatre, behind a thick wall, there were
those beds, there were those unfortunate creatures
locked up through their own aberration, there were
those women in robes whom one would sometimes
furtively pass in the corridor, and I thought that all
these subtle words in which we were going to
immerse ourselves and which were our delight and
our torment wouldn't change their condition in the
slightest, would weigh nothing in the face of their
suffering. I would sometimes find this proximity
indecent, would find unbearable the hiatus between
the genius, the charm of Lacan's thinking, the
seductiveness of his oral style, and the misery, the
distress, ignorant of all style, of the madness stored
there in the room nearby. For the room next door was
at that time, for me, not the forever re-invented one
of the mythical parents, but this room, very real and
carefully avoided, belonging to lost women. After all,
there perhaps, in that abyss of violence, was the true
location of the primal scene, and that was where we
all came from? Through the wall cries, moans,
short-lived laughter sometimes reached us.

In fact, like all of us, I had known madness, long
before attending Sainte-Anne, long before my brief visit
to Charenton. But I didn't know its name, and its forms
were more discreet. Already, in childhood, it was for
me obscurely linked to woman: madness that had been
changed into woman, or woman predestined to madness
through I know not what flaw, what internal vertigo,
what refusal also of the horrible plainness of reality. It
was different for men. We had, especially in Cabourg,
our eccentrics, our grotesques, as if they had stepped
out of an album of caricatures I'd been given for my
tenth birthday. But none of that was of much
consequence, and only elicited a smile. Maurice, for
instance, wore a wig during the day, black and smooth,
with a parting in the middle and a wave on each side,
to conceal his bald round head. If I visited him early in
the morning in his room without waiting for the ritual:
'Do come in, old chap', I could see the object reposing
on an oriental vase. Monsieur Michard was about two
metres tall and was considered to be a total idiot. The
idea that one could be both so tall and so stupid
troubled me, the me who so wished to grow up,
supported by the conviction that height and intelligence
went together (I had an older brother). Monsieur Boire,
whose name alone filled me with mirth, protruded – in
the same slow movement – his perpetually full big belly
and his ever-empty shrimping net. I would hear it said
of cousin Hubert that he was a cadger,* when *I* found
him the gentlest of men.

Nothing really worrying in these shortcomings, in

* *tapeur* = cadger; *taper* = to hit.

these innocent peculiarities, nor in the double meaning that certain words seemed to secrete. Some things were more disconcerting, which the grown-ups didn't speak about to us but which could be guessed, and a particular look on the face indicated that they had to be condemned. So-and-so 'played the horses' and incurred debts. So-and-so had a 'bird', Louis was 'fast' (another word full of mystery: from what age did speed and play turn into vices?). But, on the whole, men didn't disturb the order of the world. They went to the office every day, and the only worry one could have on their behalf was, in the end, as to whether or not they had a 'good position'. Even death, for them, didn't hide its name. They went to meet it, or it struck them – without warning but openly. I knew that many of my father's friends had died in the war; he himself had been lucky to come out of it alive, and hadn't survived a difficult operation. That's how it was with men: they departed suddenly and left a big void. What a miserable life, never to have known any merry widows!

But Louise, my grandmother, the one who had come for the summer to die in the four-windowed bedroom of her house at Cabourg – death had been in her for years. I understood it later. Since it wasn't *spoken*, I could only glimpse scattered signs which I didn't know how to bring together: she was said to be tired; my mother, whose face was more and more inscrutable, had gone with her for a few weeks to a place near the lake of Annecy, and they hadn't stayed in a hotel but in an 'establishment' with an odd name; the air was supposed to be good for her, and she had come back with a complexion greyer than the sea at Cabourg, she would

walk leaning on a cane and, that summer, it was better
not to play under her windows, better to hide our
laughter and cross the corridor by her bedroom without
a word, without a sound. From the bedroom came a
smell I couldn't define; sometimes, in the corridor, I
would pass the nurse and I thought I could see hatred
in her eyes; some days the smell became more
insistent, filtering through to other rooms in the house.
How was it that Grandmother's sunny room, how was it
that Grandmother herself, so elegant, so noble, Louise
the perfect, should smell bad? I used to jump on my
bicycle and pedal away at great speed, or else I would
work desperately for hours at running along the dunes,
as if to test my resistance and feel invulnerable.

The day the great doctor who had specially come
from Paris was asked to stay for lunch, I heard these
words: 'Nothing to be done'. After which the conversation picked up again and the sirloin wasn't any the less
good ... Once the Professor had left, my grandfather
criticized him for having charged an exorbitant fee. 'I
told him: "Monsieur, here is the amount I had prepared
for you, already considering it to be excessive." Well,
believe it or not, he accepted the note I handed him.'
We believed him. Grandfather, whom age was making
ever more sensitive and complaining, that day passed
for a hero. His gesture was acclaimed as a challenge to
the merchants of death.

'Nothing to be done': Grandmother was not only
mortal, she was going to die. I didn't know what was
making her die so slowly but, without having the least
word to designate the evil, I understood it hadn't come
from outside, that the secret which had encompassed

all these years pertained first of all to the malady itself, hidden, insidious, gradually conquering what was for me just as mysterious: the belly of an old woman.

Another bedroom in Cabourg, another woman's bedroom: Jeanne's. She was said to be 'nervous' and my grandfather, always ready to smooth away dramas, ended in advance by means of the following formula a debate which wasn't taking place: 'She is more to be pitied than blamed.' I heard this phrase so many times that for me it became a proverb, and I occasionally make use of it when animated gossip turns into self-satisfied nastiness! This sentence would leave me very perplexed, for I couldn't easily discern what might really be the reason for blame or for compassion. Yet our long stay in Cabourg was marked by Jeanne's odd ways. For her there was no respite, not a minute of holiday. These odd ways were the shadow side of our too-bright summers, they were the muffled contradiction of the exquisite politeness of the raked paths, the flowering borders, and of the happy division of labour that allowed the servants to play *une partie de bouchon**
after Sunday lunch and the masters to play tennis or golf whenever they pleased.

There again, only the repetition of some unaccustomed signs indicated to me that strange things must have been happening in Jeanne's room. From it too there filtered a particular, unpleasant smell, and there again the mystery was unveiled gradually, only to give way to a graver one. Jeanne suffered from an extravagant fear: fear of what she called microbes,

* A game similar to bowls.

invisible and uncountable enemy agents that could attack from everywhere, be transmitted by anyone. Did Jeanne wish to ward off in that way the illness that had ravaged Louise from the inside? For, against germs at least, against contamination, she could wage an incessant war, multiply her precautions, attempt to arrest suspects. The 'fifth column' was in the room: secret agents all the more efficient for being invisible were infiltrating everywhere. There wasn't a guest, a visitor who was exempt from suspicion; then, gradually, not one of the occupants of the house. Hence the investigations conducted by Jeanne or some obliging person, more or less direct enquiries, soon more and more insistent, to find out what friends we'd met, if one of them hadn't himself been in contact with someone who was ill, or had become ill since ... An endless chain: the whole world was a carrier of germs, no one alive could be innocent.

Poor Jeanne, more to be pitied than blamed, poor Jeanne who regularly had her room disinfected (that was it, the bizarre smell), this room which no one entered, not even her husband or her children, poor Jeanne who sometimes went as far as Lisieux for confession and to pray to St Theresa. Dear God, deliver us from Evil. How could I have blamed her? I found her lively, pleasantly insolent, the only really charming person in the family. To Jeanne I owe my first stirrings. I had grasped, in the course of our conversations, that she had been an adventurous, improper young woman (at any rate, in relation to the customs of the clan), that she had twice broken off engagements, ridden on horseback, travelled, worn eccentric costumes ... What a contrast with my mother, who was so prudent, my grandmother, who was so strict, both of whom, in my eyes, had always been the age they were now!

And then, without knowing it, I must have been grateful to the lovable she-devil of former times (now possessed by the devil) for disturbing the over-limpid arrangements of our summers, for grafting onto our refined rites her own sombre rituals, for celebrating her black mass while we, respectful of the proprieties and dressed all in white, would make our way to the nearby chapel in the village whose name was Home. But there was something even more disturbing: what could have changed Jeanne thus, turning a young girl endowed with so many gifts, including that of personal fortune, into this woman undermined by obsessions as one is convulsed by tics and yet still, in flashes, vibrantly imaginative? She tormented doctors, telephoning them at any time, day or night, to make sure that nothing or no one had contaminated her, that the microbes hadn't settled in this glass, in that item of underwear, and the doctors, exasperated or patient, didn't know what to do with her, totally powerless as they had also been in the face of Louise's illness. The very special Jeanne would never find her specialist. That is because she herself was an enclosed room for which no one in the world had the key.

I am glad that the words cancer and neurosis weren't available to me then. What would they have given me? Nothing, a false knowledge. Today I'm still aware of the extent to which these words and so many others serve only to mask the uncertainty one feels about one's condition, the disarray that comes from the strangeness of a way of being, the unbridgeable gulf that widens between oneself and the people one is close to. Words so as not to feel any longer, words so as not to think. It's rare nowadays to hear words which, belonging to no one in particular, can be the property of anyone, words that are solid and inexhaustible like 'grief' or 'hatred'. What then was Jeanne trying to avenge, to what unatonable hatred was she prey, to the extent of wanting to forbid impurity any access to her room? From what grief did Louise take so long to die? By what disenchantment was the garden in Cabourg taken over, summer after summer? What if it were these enigmas, posed in the absence of words and in the susceptibility to sense-impressions of the child I was, which led me many years later towards psychoanalysis?

After Cabourg, I knew other recluses and other enclosed rooms, experienced other disquieting smells. Sources mustn't be sought exclusively in the time of childhood, they can appear at any moment, unexpectedly. It's just that the unexpected, which one doesn't stop expecting, becomes rarer, and there's an incomparable flavour attached to what one believes are the original sources, as if they had appeared for you alone. Is one ever done with the *first time*?

Gilles had invited me to drop in for a visit that summer, 'if I had nothing better to do', in the Drôme where he lived all the year round. I had had a glimpse of him at the lycée ten years previously, where his reputation as an exceptionally brilliant pupil, as our teachers put it, had reached across the forms that separated us. Then lost from sight, even though living in the same *quartier*; then encountered again a few years later, by chance, coming out of a cinema, when I

was living in Montparnasse and he in the Ternes
district. He had become friendly with me then,
probably attracted by my seriousness at that time and
the fragility he sensed in it. He owned all the books,
the ones I didn't know about or didn't dare to buy. I
don't think he had read them all, don't even think he
had read any of them from cover to cover, but he had
opened them all; a sentence picked at random was
enough to set him talking for hours. His unique talent
resided in this: he invented the books of others. That
astounded me, for I used to read pen in hand, furious
when I couldn't remember, always unsure whether I
had understood, and when I had liked an author's book
I used to get all his others, perhaps less out of love than
to assure myself that this author, at least, I had done
thoroughly. Gilles's books were piled up in the greatest
disorder, spilling everywhere, even on to the floor,
guests who had lingered because they felt good there.
'Here, take this.' This was *Maldoror* or *Metamorphosis*,
Louise Labé or *Nouvelles exemplaires*, Bonaparte's
letters to Joséphine or the *Vie de Rancé*. No philosophi-
cal books at his place, nor political ones. 'How can you
be interested in those things! How boring! How
pretentious!' And he would parody Goethe: 'Theories
are grey, young man, the tree of life is always green.'
The 'young man', thus attacked in the very heart of his
projects, was extremely annoyed. He was at that time
seeking, in the study of philosophy, a rigorous order of
thought (I was preparing a thesis on Spinoza) and was
assiduously attending a Marxist group to find the logic
of History; but he had only to let himself be captured
by a novel that Gilles lent him to find imagination

queen and concepts fleshless. Back in the street – for, in the presence of Gilles, repartee deserted me – I would counter-attack: his head too was in a big mess, his literary tastes were evidence of a suspect eclecticism and, far from devouring books, he let himself be devoured by them. The tree of life certainly wasn't growing in his room in the Ternes. On the contrary I sensed a stale smell of renunciation in it, of impotence, and something like, already, an extreme weariness in this boy aged twenty-five. Besides, this great reader undoubtedly didn't write a line. I, at least, had covered a hundred and fifty pages, in dense handwriting, on substance and attribute!

Gilles lived with his mother, a widow like mine but a merrier one. Sometimes he would go off for weeks. He was evasive when he got back, almost mute, about these sudden disappearances, he who was usually so loquacious and whose monologues strayed in all directions, both fascinating and taxing me. Thus words, left to themselves, without apparent concern for their supposed recipient, could stampede, drive mad! I experienced something like vertigo. Here was Gilles – in front of me, quite close, in the room with the books, and yet in tension, kidnapped by I don't know what force of attraction – already vanished and, with him, all reality. What was he absconding from, what void unknown to himself was luring him? A flight, a vacuum that the words on show, the secret journeys didn't make good. Quite the reverse, for words were themselves running away, chasing each other and not grasping anything, and the journeys only made the not-being-there more acute.

Appointed to a post in the provinces and assured,

for my part, of having put the malady of words to such
good use as well as of having found the right distance
from the figures of the past, I had no more news of
Gilles. I only heard through a mutual acquaintance that
his mother had remarried, a man younger than herself,
and that Gilles had retired to the Drôme with, as means
of support, the meagre inheritance from his father and
what he made from his no less meagre artistic
production. For he had started to paint. 'Well,' I said, 'I
was certain he would eventually have decided to write,
especially if his mother abandoned him.' For I didn't
doubt that Gilles had felt abandoned and even betrayed
by his mother. He used to make fun of her cruelly in
my presence, but would call her for the slightest thing:
'Where did you put my green sweater?' 'Be a dear, put
the kettle on.' 'If you go out, don't forget your keys.' –
'You've no idea,' he would tell me, 'she forgets
everything. The poor thing, what would she do without
me?' It was the first real couple I had come across.

I had almost forgotten Gilles when I got a postcard
from him – a handsome portrait of a child, with a grave
expression and the look of an orphan – inviting me to
come and see him if I was ever in his area.

I left Nice at the beginning of summer, immediately
after prize-giving at which I had, as the newcomer,
made the 'usual speech'! Now it was *my* turn to correct
sentences, to plug lapses of memory, to make firm
whatever in thought was flabby; now it was me who
would be imitated at the family table, to entertain the
parents over the dessert. The good pupil had become
the good teacher, but the summer holidays remained
the summer holidays.

Halt in Avignon where the Festival was beginning, stop-over at some friends' house in the middle of fields of lavender, which set off a great purple curved sun, an emotional paying-of-respects to the palace of Monsieur Cheval the Postman and his wheelbarrow, cool drinks under the plane trees, a sweet golden-skinned girl-friend, how simple life could be, how accessible pleasures!

I had some trouble finding the house: Gilles lived at the bottom of a rocky, poorly-cultivated small valley. It was a somewhat patched-up ruin, surrounded by half-open bags of cement, broken tiles, sand, rusty bits of pipes, just left there. Materials waiting to be used, reprieved building-site, dump? A depressing picture, in any case, created less by incompleteness (which can have its charm) than by the persistence of junk, stuff one will never manage to get rid of, as if the accumulation of useless débris were the only current representation of Eternity! I found Gilles thinner but smiling, his affability somewhat forced. His books had followed him, henceforth stored soberly on shelves; and a few pieces of furniture, a rug, from his mother's flat: here I saw something like the remains of a meal he no longer shared. Other than that, nothing: a table, a wardrobe, some metal chairs. So what had happened to Gilles's refinement? He didn't show us his room. He hardly spoke during the meal, which was frugal and which we ate next to the bags of cement. My girl-friend and I were rather bewildered, she in particular, as I had described Gilles as a tireless conversationalist, a literate being from another age, an eminently discon-certing mind. 'You'll see,' I had told her, 'he's never

where you expect him.' Well, that certainly was the
case, beyond all our hopes.

In the evening Gilles left us early and retired to his
room on the first floor. I had asked to see his paintings.
'I'll show you all that tomorrow. But I know you won't
like them.' Although courteous with my girl-friend –
'Do you like curd cheese?' – he acted as if she weren't
there. She and I went to bed in a big bed, it was a
beautiful, welcoming night. We didn't dare touch each
other. Besides, did we want to? I was awakened a few
hours later – probably Gilles's footsteps up above – and
immediately assailed by a smell I couldn't identify. The
smell of coffee in the morning, signalling the start of a
new day which might be happy, didn't banish it. Gilles
only turned up at the end of the morning, unshaven,
dull-eyed.

In the afternoon, I saw his paintings which he got
out from a corner of the vast attic above his room. An
ordeal for the painter, probably even more for the
witness. What to say? 'You're wrong: I like them very
much.' (Silence.) 'This one, maybe a bit less' (insult).
'That, is that the hill behind the house?' – 'No, that has
nothing to do with it.' – 'When did you paint that one?'
– 'Why do you ask?' – 'I had the feeling it was more
recent ... I mean less ...' I floated a formula that fell
flat: hallucinatory realism. Fortunately Gilles seemed to
accept my idiocies with indifference. Then we went for
a walk. I inquired about the few inhabitants of the
valley. Thereupon he recovered his talent as a
story-teller, revealing their secrets, inventing their lives
as, formerly, he'd invented books. Still affected by the
paintings he had just shown me, I listened to him

absentmindedly, rather ungraciously, as if my gaze might tear bits of flesh off him. No doubt the paintings were not terribly accomplished, their 'technique' left much to be desired, but there was something intense and truthful in them. For a long time I had found the forced distinction between abstract and figurative painting precarious and even absurd: one can very well, I would say to myself, make a triangle figurative, make a lamp or a bunch of flowers abstract, make its particular essence appear through and in what is perceptible, especially if one does such a simple thing as letting oneself be convinced by its complexity. That, it seemed to me, was what Gilles was clumsily, stubbornly, engaged in. He painted a tuft of grass, or an old wall, until he had exhausted it, and it was, as it sometimes is in a dream, the opposite of vague: the presence, without any distance, of the naked thing! Still somewhat imbued with Spinoza, I thought (if only to lighten the weight of that day, the sad failure of our reunion): in the attribute he's looking for the substance! He's tidied up his books, he's shelved them as one disposes of a piece of work one has abandoned, because he has realized that words, which only go from substitute to substitute and only bring to life a shadow that calls forth another shadow, would never give him this elusive substance. I wasn't entirely on the wrong track, but I was mistaken all the same.

I realized it that night when I went into his room, narrow and enclosed like a chapel, with images reminiscent of ex-votos on its whitewashed walls. I saw him lying on his bed, smoking something – I don't know what – absorbing it with an extreme attention so as to become totally impregnated by it and dissolve in that absorption. On a small table next to him he had carefully laid out a whole paraphernalia to celebrate his worship. It looked as if he were paying homage to some unknown god. So that was it, the substance. 'They fobbed off some disgusting stuff on me,' Gilles said. 'I've no money left to get anything good.' He didn't tell me what it was he was smoking and I didn't ask. I heard myself utter words deriving from mother, grandmother, great-grandmother: 'You're crazy, you're going to ruin your health.' Gilles heard nothing. I think that I stayed there for a moment looking at him, observing his not being there, repeating to myself like an idiot: I've found the smell, the smell of the substance. Then I left the enclosed room.

Since then I've never again heard mention of Gilles.

Toxicomania, a medical word. Is it true that the drug addict is infatuated with the poison and only wants to destroy himself? What if what he is looking for were a state in which the fusion with substance was at last possible? And what if the poison is in fact what *we* are prey to: the impurity of signs? I see them, Jeanne and Gilles, those two recluses, I see them, I who prudently stay on *terra firma*, endlessly drifting on their raft, enervated like the two young people of Jumièges whose punishment was to be sent floating down the Seine, their nerve fibres cut.

Rooms in old provincial hotels, in Andalusia, in Tuscany, with green shutters closed from the morning onwards, which Claire and I came to, dead tired in the evenings, and where we slipped under clean sheets after a shower. Mirrored rooms in a brothel, expressly made for the ephemerality of bodies. The poorly-heated room at the end of the corridor where, wrapped in woollens, I prepared for exams and tests, dreaming of something other. My mother's room, overlooking a dark courtyard, my mother who had such difficulty smiling on the succession of days. Children's rooms, peopled with games, with painted images, a desert where no plant will grow after the children have gone. A hospital room where, a few weeks ago, I went to visit an old friend who will never come out. And today this room in which I have shut myself up. No, now I'm cheating: the small window is wide open. I see in the garden, between tall blades of grass, the yellow beak of the blackbird, the stones of the wall under the brambles; beyond, the meadow; further still, sails on the sea and the sea comes into the garden and the blackbird flapping his wings changes into a white gull heavier in its flight. Yes, the window remains wide open during the hours when I write. I need free space, a sky that breathes at every moment. I must have air to dream my memory.

Look, an expansive flight of swallows. How I wish that my words, assured of their place of origin and of being able to return there, were migratory birds!

9 The big Other*

Sartre at Pasteur in 1941, Lacan at Sainte-Anne in 1954. What luck to have known them both in their beginnings, before the glory of their name preceded – and concealed – them ...

With Sartre, there was neither difficulty nor merit in proving my incapacity for allegiance. Sartre – it was probably due as much to his pride as to his wish to be just like 'anyone else', without land and without possessions, without legacy and without legatees – didn't tolerate anybody following in his footsteps. No reverence nor reference: can one imagine him speaking of 'his teaching'? He was happy only in contradiction, but contradiction directed towards himself. Since he didn't acknowledge any father, he wasn't going to encumber himself with any sons, who would be just as dependent in rebellion as in submission. For a while, after the lycée years, I used to call him jokingly 'my old master' and he was a little embarrassed even by this affectionate mockery. As for Lacan (everyone knows this), he volunteered to uphold the vacant position of Master – at the time a word, a function, totally suspect to me: here self-infatuation and abuse of power came together, the knowingly maintained illusion of withholding (and keeping for oneself) the key

* *Le Grand Autre.*

words and a supreme contempt for followers. Besides, I
thought, who, without laughing, would let himself be
called 'dear Master'? Mallarmé, but also Anatole France,
Sacha Guitry. And what exactly would one be master of:
of Zen? of fencing? of passions or of slaves? I distrusted
the word, smelling as it simultaneously did of sects, of
fin-de-siècle drawing-rooms, and of tyranny. I gradually
learned to recognize the fear that this distrust fed on.
Wanting at all costs to keep my father inside me – as if,
having nothing then any longer to fear from him, I could
thus have nothing to fear from anyone else – no doubt
anything evoking the idea of a change of father was out of
bounds for me. And also, if one had to suffer, I preferred
it to be through women.

There were relatively few of us throughout the fifties –
just over a hundred attending the Seminar. And that, of
course, added to the pleasure; of different educational
backgrounds and ages, we came from everywhere, with no
specific aim, our only certainty that of going, each by his
own path, to a personal appointment on Wednesdays at
twelve-fifteen. We knew from an indubitable source,
since we were at the source of a new way of thinking and
of a hitherto unknown way of speaking, that an event was
taking place there. What event? I would have been
hard-pressed to define it, the more so since nothing had
prepared me for it, which is precisely what made it an
event: something was happening, was happening to me. I
had known excellent teachers at Pasteur, some less good
ones in Khâgne. At the Sorbonne, I had been bored: my
mind was often somewhere else, more often nowhere.
Even Bachelard hadn't really captivated me. I preferred
the inventive vigour and the flavour of his books to his

somewhat spluttering, disordered speech, and above all I
preferred my solitary room to a class-room. To come close
to a thought, to palpate its solidity, to grasp its contents,
who needed commentators or interpreters? It's the palate
that counts when one tastes a fruit. When I became a
teacher in my turn, I told myself that my job had one aim
only: to teach my pupils to read. Apart from that, since it
was also necessary to satisfy the requirements of the
course, I liked clarity, concise formulas, precise statements. Success in coping with the most daunting questions in a manner that was lively and used everyday
language would put me in good spirits for the day.

But Lacan, after having slowly laid out on the chair
papers he never consulted, books he didn't open, after
having wiped the lenses of his spectacles for several
minutes and having cast over the assembly a gaze that
he endeavoured to make as gloomy as possible – as if it
were really beyond his powers to address such a
collection, less of ignoramuses than of blocked-up ears,
even if it was often Jean Hyppolite or Merleau-Ponty
who were lending theirs in the front row ... – Lacan
then would sigh, seized by an immense weariness,
would begin to emit a few sounds, exhaling in a first or
last breath – was he about to collapse or take wing,
leave us in the lurch right there, or never stop? – words
barely audible at first, punctuated by much clearing of
his throat; suddenly the voice would rise, become
stronger, the flow would quicken, his gaze would now
be fixing us but still as if despairing of ever waking us
up to what he was addressing; sometimes he would
apostrophize us directly: 'So, are you going to open
them up now, your brain-boxes! When will you begin to

understand the first thing about what I've been working myself into the ground to teach you all these years?' and, thus re-launched, he would wrap us in sentences that rarely had an end – each taking the baton from the previous unfinished one, to a different rhythm and on another track – which the most zealous among us strove to transcribe in large exercise-books. With Lacan, thought always appeared to unfold outside his theme, describing a never-ending spiral: one could never tell whether this was taking us away from or bringing us closer to the centre. Lacan or the art of suspense.

Where were we? Certainly not in a class-room. At the theatre, in some temple? At Mesmer's, at Gurdjieff's? With the prince of sophists corrupting the young? None of these. Here all analogies would be misleading. For Lacan, while he employed – unknowingly, so natural was it to him – the resources of the actor and the talents of the magus, in no way played with the seductions of paradox or the prestige of mystery. His passion for speaking wasn't feigned. Speech was indeed in suspense, in abeyance, pending, moving forward through digressions, parentheses, side-steps and abrupt break-throughs towards ever greater exactitude. Lacan sinned more through excess of rationalism than through indulgence in the irrational. The unconscious wasn't his god but his object of study. And like all rationalists, he loved argument and, like all passionate beings, showed not the least respect for his adversary. We liked that at a time – which is now returning – when so many psychoanalysts were in search of legitimacy. A bit of Lacan's ardour fell on us. Half a century on from Freud, we could think of ourselves as the first Freudian circle: better still – as those who had truly read, truly understood Freud. The first time – the true time, which isn't necessarily the first chronologically – was us. We had, as a bonus, the feeling that we were indispensable to Lacan, that, even if we rarely intervened during the Seminar and only when he asked us to, we made it possible for him to say what without us would never have come into the world. Yes, I believe that this conviction, not as mad as it seems, kept us going. It was like a constant exchange of roles: he was our analyst and we were his patients as well as his audience; each of us, being sensitive above all to the effect produced on us by what we heard, was his analyst and he was our patient. Sometimes a ludicrous thought passed through us: what would have become of him without our collaboration? Deliberately mute, delirious perhaps ... A part of the event consisted of that as well.

Often, after the Seminar, which finished a bit later every time, I went to have coffee with a friend. 'So, what did he have to say today, your Lacan?' As she knew me to be generally more prompt with criticism than fervour, she was disconcerted by my assiduity. How could I answer her? Sometimes I did have a few formulae for her to get her teeth into: 'To love is to give what one doesn't have', or again (love being at that time my main interest): 'Love is a pebble laughing in the sun.' I could see my friend brooding. But she was also extremely knowledgeable; I therefore had to report less enigmatic 'utterances', as they were called at the time. I explained to her the primacy of the signifier over the signified ('But that's Saussure'), that the ego was not subject but object, that its function was to do with the imaginary ('But that's in Sartre and even in La Rochefoucauld'). I praised the symbolic order as that

which constitutes us, the lived is a cock-up ('But that's
Lévi-Strauss'), I showed her the point of speaking about
metaphor and metonymy rather than condensation and
displacement ('But that's Jakobson'), I put it to her that
the real name for the death instinct was entropy ('But
that's Freud'). Growing tired of this war, I told her,
irritated, that it was absurd to reduce Lacan to his
utterances, that he was utterly in the articulations of his
own thought and, as to that, she would have to hear him
for herself and could only be convinced if she were
prepared to give up what, as the result of an excessively
prolonged stay at university, she believed she knew.
'That's the typical response of the disciple,' Simone
retorted: ' "Draw nigh unto the Master, hearken to his
holy word and thou shalt understand." For the disciple,
truth always comes from the other's mouth.' – 'Precisely,'
I told her, 'Lacan refers to the Other, with a big O,* he
doesn't claim to capture its place, even less to fill it.' She
considered me lost, and I imagined her murmuring: 'Poor
soul, he's more to be pitied than blamed!' She blamed my
blindness *vis-à-vis* Lacan and my belligerence *vis-à-vis*
herself on the transference, and the most alienating
transference of all, she added – the one that's never
worked through. 'It would be a good idea if you re-read
Group Psychology and the Analysis of the Ego.'

It so happened that on the day when we had this
caustic exchange I took Simone to a music-hall in
which there appeared someone called 'le Grand
Robert'. He was a handsome man in evening dress who
had come from Quebec to hypnotize the boulevard

* *avec un grand A.*

crowds. In fact that evening, as summer was drawing near, there were not many in the audience, a little fewer than at the Seminar. The demonstration wasn't going too well. To lift his failing show and give assurance of his powers, *le Grand Robert* had the idea of inviting the spectators to come up on stage. Bravely we went up. Other members of the audience had already preceded us, all from the front rows, and we told ourselves that we were most certainly the only ones, among the candidates for hypnosis, not to have been recruited as stooges.

Relax, look at me, look at nothing else, no one else, look at me, stare into my eyes, take deep breaths, deep breaths, now close your eyes, you have closed your eyes, deep breaths, deeeep ... breaths. You are asleep. We followed *le Grand Robert*'s injunctions to the letter. It went on for several minutes. I took the liberty of opening one eye: I caught a glimpse next to me of a young man frozen in the catatonic rigidity that I had observed at Sainte-Anne; it seemed to me that Simone was slightly unsteady. The man in evening dress had lost his calm, he no longer controlled the melody of his solemn voice, his Canadian accent was becoming downright comic, he was sweating. The lordly magician had turned into nothing more than a monkey-tamer, furious because the monkeys won't jump through the hoop. Try as I might to breathe deeper and deeper, there was nothing doing. Two characters suddenly sprang up from backstage and roughly ejected me. Without waiting for more, Simone slipped away. After which, the show continued. Back in our seats, slightly sheepish, we could see the accomplices – or (after all, why not?) subjects less resistant to suggestion than ourselves – docilely obey the orders of *le Grand Robert*. He had them do a few dance-steps, he had them embrace, and he even got one of them to cross the stage on all fours, with another one on his back in the guise of a jockey. The men were spinning under umbrellas, the women grimacing under clownish hats. The idea came to me that it was in order to take revenge on us that he humiliated them in this way.

On leaving the Olympia as one emerges from a bad dream, Simone and I were certainly not in a laughing mood. No, of course, *le Grand Jacques* wasn't *le Grand Robert*: a blasphemous, absurd thought – still, I had had to push it away. But what if the latter were the vulgar, sinister caricature of the former, as the brothel is the dark face of the salon where the *beaux esprits* sparkle? What if, in the final analysis, they used the same means to exercise their hold? And, above all, what if it were the same sensitive point that they touched in each of us? Thus it was that on my internal dissecting-table disinterested chance had brought together Doctor Jacques Lacan's sewing-machine and the false Doctor Robert's umbrella. I spent an agitated night. The following Wednesday, Simone was at the Seminar. And, long after I had stopped attending it, she was still going.

One can accept anything from an exceptional person. Each peculiarity enhances him. But to glimpse his reflection in others reduces his value. Week after week, the epidemic was spreading. The multiplication of bow-ties and cigars was one thing. The following season, with a bit of luck, other 'unitary traits' would do. But the sighs and inhalations, but the allusive formulas and the smugness of the smiles, but my poor friend Jean-Pierre, simple-hearted and balding, who was spending a fortune at Carita's because, according to rumour, Lacan had his mane coiffed there! I had nothing against Lacan for his mannerisms and eccentricities, his *grand seigneur* caprices. Rather, they intrigued and amused me. I even saw in them something like an illustration of that unconscious whose features he outlined for us via *Der Witz** and the dream of Irma's injection: eccentric, in a word, this bloody Ucs, and baroque and calculating and invincibly cocky. No, what distressed me was to note that, if we really had to imitate our Master or go through this 'imaginary identification' in spite of its having been so often denounced, we did it so badly – and I included myself in this 'we', because in wanting to dissociate oneself from the herd one still bears the brand of the shepherd. What is Lacan's intention, I wondered: to convey to us some idea of a big Other, perhaps nameless and assuredly faceless, yet here we were attempting to ape the small other, as if we were still captured by an image and arrested at a mirror phase, but a mirror phase far from always jubilant!

Thought never arouses only interest, it arouses passion, and it's never thought alone that is involved. It is deeply imbued with a way of speaking, a tone, wholly animated by a voice. It has a body which, like each body, is unique, a body that we want to possess from the moment it attracts us, in the mad hope of knowing it

* Freud's *Jokes and their Relation to the Unconscious.*

at last. Especially when thought is presented orally, it
stops offering itself – supposing this were ever possible
anyway – as an object that one might observe from
outside, taking apart its components and comparing
them with others. The more one tries to seize it, the
more one is seized by it, to the point of mimesis. And
the more thought hides, the more attracted we are, as to
a desired woman, to the point of believing that if we
were suddenly deprived of it and no longer had it (even
fugitively) before our eyes, we would lose not only all
thought but all existence. It sometimes happens that
what is most alien to us, most radically *other*, is the one
thing which is our own.

Lacan made me break with academic habits to
which even Sartre in his abrupt ways remained, despite
everything, loyal. 'I've told you what I think about the
issue. Now it's up to you to place your bets ... or
blows.' For in my eyes Sartre was as much that small,
stocky and determined man who had practised boxing
when he was young as he was the natural incarnation of
the Cogito. As for Lacan, who moved always leaning
forward and slightly swaying, as if it were an
intolerable concession to vulgar stupidity to hold
oneself upright and walk straight, I imagined him
rather as handling a foil, as a malicious expert in the
art of fencing. As far as the Cogito is concerned and its
proud and confident certainty, he turned it inside-out
like a glove: *I do not think in the place where I am, I
am not in the place where I think.* A proposition to
which I associated as an echo, probably in order to
lessen its disastrous implications for myself, the words
of a song by Yvonne Printemps that my mother used to

hum: *I am not what they think, I am not what they say.*
To each his ideal, to each his season ... For my part, I
looked to the bat for help: *I am a bird, see my wings, I
am a mouse, long live rats*!

To feed on Lacan, to stay in Lacania without talking
Lacanian: a probably impossible task to which I
nevertheless buckled down. For several years I published
accounts of the Seminar, I wrote about Lacan in words
that weren't his. I was no doubt mistaken to attempt it: in
my eagerness to 'translate' him I revealed my reluctance
to 'incorporate' him. I was no doubt afraid: afraid that, if I
allowed the impregnation to proceed, I would dissolve
into smoke like Gilles in his closed room. But I can see
quite well what then drove me: the refusal, not to
recognize my debt, which remains immense, to his person
and his thinking, but to be caught in his *langue*. For I
could see Lacan gradually forging his *langue* by means of
successive torsions, and around me the disciples, the
people next to me, being converted without even realizing
it (and that above all was odious to me). Some have never
found their way out of that enclosure, which governs all
the others. Having never really got in, either as bird or as
mouse, it would be ungracious of me, as the unforgettable
little other of the past put it, to pity them or blame them.

It is, after all, the prayer and fate of the greatest to
create their own *langue*, to flush out its hidden meaning
and make it leap away, like a hare. Where harm comes in
is when that new *langue* seeks to impose itself. It then
ends up, contrary to its initial destiny, ordaining the
words of the tribe. There is tyranny in its claim to say
what is, in these particular words. I came to think that

only a shared* *langue* gives speech a chance, allows it to come through in its uniqueness. Speech is tyrannical too, but open to all meanings. That is because it doesn't know where it comes from and where it is going. It is without god or master.

Once a week, Lacan conducted a case-presentation, also at Sainte-Anne. The woman whom the house-doctor proposed one day for his enquiry complained of being followed: she was followed everywhere, in the street, in shops, and even at home. Lacan, always extremely civil with mental patients, concluded the interview thus: 'Madame, don't worry. I shall find someone here to *follow* your progress.' Lacan, betrayed, like each of us, by himself, by the *langue*, transformed despite himself into a follower of his own axiom, *It*** *speaks*: of this particular Lacan I preserve an intact and smiling memory.

*commune.
**Ça = *das Es*, the id.

10 The fall of bodies

I saw Charles Lindbergh cross the Atlantic in the Châtelet theatre.

I saw a man throw himself, smiling, from the top of the Eiffel Tower. He was wearing big wings. He had summoned journalists and cinematography. His fall was in a straight line. He crashed at the feet of officials in dark suits. I don't know his name. He was called the Bird Man. He had left no chance to chance as regards the preparations for his exploit.

Several times a year, I see in my sleep aeroplanes of considerable size dive in free fall, as if naturally, into the small wood at the end of the garden at Boissy.

We have invented words in order to escape from the law of gravity, in order to delay the fatal moment of the fall.

11 Margins

What does the sack of memory hold – the sack which is so full of holes? Accidents. We think it is our memory that assures us a certain continuity, when in fact it is because of our *body* that, in spite of everything, in spite of separations, disorders, changes of all kinds, we are able to recognize this life as our own, to derive actions, emotions and thoughts from the same point and relate them to the same pronoun 'I', to go so far sometimes as to confuse the world with our gaze on it. In fact, in our memory, we find only the *dis*continuous: namely, events, important for us but most often infinitesimal, wounds (and a wound always leaves some invisible trace), moments of turmoil, hollows and excesses. Memory is what stands out, affording contrast, and the poorest memory is never completely flat.

Shapeless sack or else photographic plate sensitive to the slightest oscillation of time, jumble of archives where the essential document and the scribbled gibberish mingle and endlessly go over the same confused business, room bolted against the void or vast coloured space crossed by roads, darkened by forests, irrigated by rivers and lakes like a geographical map: I have the most contradictory images of memory. True, in the accidents along the route I encounter what is unique, but true too that in my memory I gather up the everyday, the repeated.

On getting up, I like the shower, which – by the grace of water – gives me back a skin and promptly drags me out of the limbo of night; then coffee at the counter – 'Strong?' – 'Yes, nice and strong, thank you, Pierre'; then good morning to little Choupette and Dame Gisou when I collect my mail in the Rue Sébastien-Bottin. The accidental, in this beginning of my days, would be for these innocent habits to be absent. I know that when I shall have forgotten the hundreds of manuscripts read, the books published, the faces of authors met, I shall be left with these habits. What certainty, what trust do they embody for me, so that, once I'm assured they haven't stood me up, I move with a quicker and calmer step, carrying deep within me the illusion of knowing where I'm heading? I sense that, deprived of these small signs of life that are, one says, insignificant, I would wander like a lost soul in search of an abode; I would then hasten to find other such signs of life to fulfil the same function. Children need their mother to tuck them in and kiss them before they are willing to go to sleep. Well, I need the baptism of the shower, the communion of the counter and the smile of the two guardian angels of the mail before I agree to wake up! But I don't wish to lose entirely the shadows of the night.

I find it impossible to write without leaving, there, on the left, a margin that I like to be unmistakable and very wide, but, on the right, not the slightest bit of white and, between the two, letters huddled body to body. The lines and the margin thus separated by an invisible frontier make the journey possible; everyone, beginning with myself, can stroll freely over the page. But in life, where can one find the text inscribed in the flow of days, where is the margin? Text and margin exchange places when an interval of time creates a hollow. Curiously, there appears to me just now an affinity between my habits of today and some of my activities of the past whose main attraction was to break with habits. Located at that time in the margin, they now come to the foreground, no longer as accidents along the route but as tracing, on the contrary, a route in which I recognize myself better than elsewhere. While I was a student I worked for a few months as a radio announcer; while I was a teacher, I was an amateur actor; and, as a psychoanalytic novice, to distract myself from the feeling of imposture which then invaded me as I observed a deep silence in my deep armchair, I opened my door to visitors much more incongruous than my patients. But, as it turned out, there was nothing deep or heavy in all this; and, if imposture there were, it was up to me to uncover it in them.

A psychologist as to whose competence and serious-ness I was in no doubt had suggested that I see, for 'in depth' (again ...) interviews, young people of both sexes applying for a fairly large grant which would allow them to fulfil their vocations. The idea was to evaluate the authenticity of that declared vocation, its consistency, its chances for the future. No test or questionnaire, no, simply a conversation. I accepted the offer with pleasure. At last an examination without rules, without a pro-gramme and without consequences (I understood that a superior agency took the decisions), which brought face to face for a few hours two strangers, both equally ignorant of what was to be the agenda of the meeting and the behaviour to adopt. My advantage, if it were one, was to be protected from any crafty questions concerning my recent Freudian vocation.

Innumerable pottery candidates, sheep-rearing candidates; only slightly more rare, model-builders reconstructing ('Two years' work, Monsieur') piece by piece some Royal Navy galley; and that enthusiast of *bel canto* who had come from Toulouse just for the occasion in a new white suit with red stripes and a head of dyed wavy hair, who, without stage fright, sang me a Verdi aria; and that terribly sad young woman, whose only dream was to re-educate the handicapped; then more potters, ceramicists, shepherds, the poet and his slim volume, the violinist and his violin, the painter and his gouaches, and even, once, a philosopher who, although born in La Flèche,* idolized Teilhard de Chardin. I listened to them, marvelling at such assurance, often astounded by such silliness, finding again in each interview the same pattern: it hardly mattered to me whether this was invented to make their cause carry conviction. In order to have one's vocation recognized, three conditions had to be fulfilled: it must have been apparent since childhood; must have been successively thwarted by parents, school and environment; must have emerged more urgent than ever, reinforced by all the frustrations and obstacles. Most often they didn't know how to speak about it, they lacked eloquence just as they were destitute of diplomas and degrees, and that is why they brought me their violin or poem as exhibits. Shall I confess that I was more touched

*Descartes, when young, was a pupil of the college at La Flèche.

by these uneducated and slightly nutty, self-taught
people than by my sober pupils of the past, or even by the
no less sober neurotics of my couch, whose favourite
culture, these last – but as if they were wedded to it! –
was only their own symptoms, made by them into a coat of
arms?

What touched me in my visitors was not so much
their somewhat forced conviction or their commissioned
passion as their bungling. Yes, they were bunglers with
words. Not only because in the main they expressed
themselves poorly, clumsily, but because the difficulty
they experienced in putting their enthusiasm into words
was only the consequence of a more general incapacity.
I thought, when faced with them, of gatherings of what
are called ordinary people that I had attended sometimes: a meal for a wedding or communion, when they
have gone to a lot of trouble, the food is plentiful,
starched napkins and table-cloth have been pulled out
of the cupboard, they want to honour the newly-weds or
the little one, family and friends are all there, one
drinks and stuffs oneself, even the sun participates,
apparently nothing is lacking. Laughter explodes between the leg of lamb and the *bombe glacée*, then
heavily falls away: the only thing missing is conversation. A game of *boules* comes in handy to save the day
while the women are already busy clearing up. Aimless
conversation, what a luxury! How delightful it can be to
speak in order to say nothing and to say everything, in
a lively, bantering, unconsidered exchange, in which
the words of one person endlessly deflect the words of
the other and yet unwind the same invisible thread.
Disgruntled people complain when they get home: 'We

didn't talk about anything, we only touched the surface.' But what if that were free speech, if that were
language at its most likeable: to be just aimless, and to
pass from mouth to mouth without *fixing* anywhere?
Whereas, with my candidates, I was dealing only with
fixed ideas.

I could think of them as ridiculous monomaniacs,
lonely people sick with pride, but I could just as well
consider them (hence the emotion I still feel when I
summon them up) as marginalized creatures, exiled from
the interior, like those ordinary people celebrating. For
they were not just excluded from the art of conversation,
that adult equivalent of children's games, but from the
whole endless dialogue that society conducts with itself
and in which we are the speakers without even realizing
it. I imagined them, my candid candidates, having come
from families crushed by silence, having gone through
schools where their homework was punctuated in the
margin by incredulous exclamations – 'incoherent',
'absurd' – but as too docile to swell the class-rooms of
problem or maladjusted children; I imagined them facing
judges who condemned them without their even knowing
what their crime was and turning to the person next to
them to see if he wasn't the guilty party instead, as I had
seen happen in the past when, on my way back from the
Sorbonne, I stopped at the Law Courts; I saw them having
their turn stolen at counters of the Post Office or Social
Security, getting the wrong train, date, epoch ..., more lost
in life than I had been occasionally – but only for a few
days or a few hours when I'd been possessed by a single
certainty, that nothing and no one was waiting for me or,
worse still, that no one in the world could give me the

least support. Only their *idée fixe*, to which the word
vocation gave a heroic colouring, was likely to fix them, to
put an end to their vague errings, to give a solidity to their
shapeless existence. A Provençal bowl, a flock of sheep, a
model, a disabled body to rehabilitate, at least that had a
shape.

But something bothered me in connection with them:
how to decide if one project was acceptable, another
valueless? Certainly, in principle, the question wasn't my
business, I should be limiting myself to gauging their
character ... Still, the question posed itself and it still
does when I hear certain psychoanalytic colleagues
intone the psalm to creativity and make of each of us a
little demiurge. I accept that all men are equal, but not
that there is no hierarchy of their productions. And I get
into a rage when a suitcase or pair of trousers that I am
going to buy carries the label of their 'creator'. When I
was finished with the vocational candidates, I decided
permanently to banish from my vocabulary the word
'creative', and I dreamt of an aesthetic which knows,
when holding forth on inventive genius, how to establish
the difference between a rose and a dandelion, even if I
don't like roses, between *The Magic Flute* and the
'singing fool',* even if Trenet enchants me.

Anything that can sharpen, renew, enlarge the idea we
make of reality merits our responsiveness, anything that
can free us from adherence and, in the first place, from
adherence of name to thing. To earn a few *sous*, I went,
the year I attained my majority, to philosophize in a minor
key at a crammer. The Fides college, then in its infancy,

* La Flute enchantée *et le fou chantant.*

was located in the family apartment of its director; I
officiated in the dining-room, sometimes in the kitchen.
There, with no vocation to transfigure failure, were
mocking daddy's boys who, when I cited for them a *pensée*
of Pascal or some aphorism by Nietzsche, consented to
emerge for a moment from their half-sleep: 'That one
would look quite good on an ashtray.' Such was the tribute
they paid to my felicitous knowledge. To reach the Fides
college, I got off at Pigalle; in the street, I passed
nonchalant American soldiers, laughing prostitutes, and
the black giants of the Military Police. Go and be earnest
about Kantian ethics after that! My mission accomplished, I would hang out in a bar where someone played
the piano. New York in Pigalle, Kant alongside the
whores, the apprentice philosopher among the nincom-
poops and a post-war period when everything was
permitted: I was in seventh heaven. In my family of origin
– one finds others in the course of life, until the eventual
recognition that one belongs to that first one – it was
considered better not to wear anything *mismatched*: it was
bad taste or, worse, vulgar. To sport an apple-green tie
with a blue shirt was more than an offence against the
harmony of colours, it was to commit a misalliance. In
order that the world might be *comme il faut*, it was
necessary to ensure above all that things went on being
exactly the same. Colours had to match each other, men
marry young women of their own milieu, and words and
gestures suit the circumstances.

However, if some recollections have remained accessible to me, isn't it because they are badly matched
with my memory, because they confuse the image I
have of myself today? Mismatched recollections, like

the one of Fides-Pigalle. At that time I liked the disharmony between my job and the décor, between the Rue Lepic and the good neighbourhoods, between my curiosity, free from all vocation, and the apathy of my audience of dunces. As it happened, all the dunces passed their exams. Long live the mismatched, and metaphysical children, and my unstable youth, melancholic and carefree, studious and frivolous, and those women who never stay the same!

Pleasure can often be found, like an object discovered at the flea-market, in small temporary jobs. The following year brought me another one. I heard that the French Broadcasting Corporation was recruiting staff. By means of a competitive exam: the Republic was back among us. This time I had to surmount the most ingeniously organized obstacles I have ever known. The *agrégation*, later, seemed to me an unbelievably congruous pushover. First some pretty crude traps were laid for us. On a typed sheet – resurgence of the H régime – sentences to be completed, illegible words that had to be read, unpronounceable words that had to be said straight out into the microphone or even blunders that the presence of mind of the candidate was supposed to correct on the spot. 'You have just heard, broadcast from the Comédie-Française, *On ne badine pas avec l'amour* by Paul Claudel.' How many, out of too much respect for the sheet, were victims of this trick! Others attempted a compromise: by Paul de Musset.* And it was necessary to think fast, again as in the H school, but of course I had grown up since then: I frustrated all the ruses, slipped

* *Alfred* de Musset is the author of *One Doesn't Trifle with Love*.

through the obstacles and was declared ready for the next
test, which was a treat. As we were supposed, if accepted,
to be able to present the most varied programmes, the
exercise consisted of finding the right tone for the
particular kind of programme; we had to prove, in five
minutes, our skill in accomplishing all the routines, in
doing all the voices: breathless, like the sports commenta-
tor reporting live the progress of the Tour de France;
serene, a bit cold, like the news-reader; playful and
cordial like the announcer of a variety show; imbued with
delicate nuances for a poetry reading: 'Gwendolen, as she
made her way through the forest, came upon the affrighted
deer ...' This time it was the recitation test that I thought I
had got back to, where the whole skill lay in adopting 'the
right tone' and where, if one wasn't afraid to arouse the
sarcasm of one's class-mates, one had every chance of
coming first. I came first! Short-lived triumph. A
producer of programmes glorifying victorious France
decided that I lacked the necessary grandiloquence: one
doesn't trifle with broadcasting. A planner of concert
programmes in whose presence I had mispronounced
'Dvorak' and 'Peer Gynt' had instantly spotted my lack of
musical culture. I was placed in the *Sound Screen* (?) of
Rue Armand-Moisant, regretfully it seemed to me, a bit as
an officer cadet whom they would have liked to see win
fame in a fighter squadron might have been appointed to
the Army Service Corps. That spot suited me down to the
ground. My task was, literally, that of stop-gap:* my
mouth stopped being shut only if there were gaps in the
programme. Should some unfortunate 'technical hitch'

* *bouche-trou.*

occur, a red bulb lit up on my table: it was up to me. I
would then announce to the dear listeners, as they were
still called at the time, that normal service would be
resumed in a moment and I would play a few records, to
help them curb their impatience. After which, very
comfortable in my studio, I would resume the thread of
my erudite studies. Sometimes – this was my greatest
moment of glory – I used to replace the Speaking Clock
when it happened to break down. A glance at my watch,
which had a will of its own, and I announced
peremptorily: 'At the fourth stroke, it will be exactly
seven twenty-seven and fifteen seconds.' Employees,
rebuked on those days by superiors for inexplicable
lateness, commuters forgotten on their station platform,
lovers driven mad by waiting, forgive me and never again
trust clocks that speak through my mouth. In spite of all
its advantages – I was well paid, in my padded cell I
could devote myself to the Stoics much better than in the
Sainte-Geneviève library – the job didn't have many
surprises in store for me. The time is exactly ... You are
now going to hear ... I thought it witty to link the two bits
of information: 'Although it is exactly seven minutes past
six in the morning, you are going to hear "Tango in
Moonlight".'   Or: 'It is freezing cold today. Let us
therefore listen to "Burning Andalusia".' My boss didn't
appreciate this innovation, and I took his comments as a
pretext for leaving the muffled studio there and then and
without too much regret. I had learned to play with my
voice: that was useful for the exams I passed at the end of
the year and, since then, in many other circumstances ...

One thinks one recollects words when in fact it's
only the intonations that inflicted a wound or served as

balm. But, mixed with the ludicrous during my stay in
Rue Armand-Moisant, a vague disquiet surfaces: what if
I myself, when I believe I'm speaking in my own right,
were only a radio set, what if, when I want to make my
voice heard, it were all the voices I've heard – repeated, altered – passing through my announcer's
mouth, what if I were, if we all were, only 'sound
screens'?

What self-denial more effective, for someone who
wants to be himself, than the gift of mimicry! Thus one
preserves a possibility, through conscious imitation and
the deliberate accentuation of the model's traits, of not
being the mere echo of admired voices. I'm nearly sure
of not being the involuntary replica of the few people I
know how to imitate – I shan't say who they are.

I dreamt of being an actor. Character parts in
particular appealed to me, big or small, from Molière to
Labiche. Nothing like make-believe, nothing like pretence, nothing like from time to time being an actor for
exorcizing the actor in oneself. To go on stage and in that
well-circumscribed space, the time of a performance, to
give shape, demeanour, voice to the thousands of little
others embedded in us. The naturalness that we envy in
some children goes together with their taste for disguises,
for play, for clowning. We might meet fewer puppets in
life if a period of time – I was going to say a *retreat* – in
the theatre were compulsory. Once, but that's not enough,
I acted in Alexandria, where my mission was the
spreading of French culture. With an amateur company, I
had to direct a '*pièce rose*' by Anouilh. I forget its title, but
the turn of events has stayed with me. A rather attractive
girl, very reserved, had the leading part. Was it the girl,

Nicole Angel, or her angelic rôle that attracted me? In
any case, I found her partner atrocious. I picked another
one, equally bad, and manoeuvred cunningly enough for
the company itself to ask me, a few days before the
performance, to replace the young lover at short notice.
Preserving my privileges as director, I gave priority to the
actor's. Little Angel and myself would slowly, silently,
walk towards one another, each starting from the opposite
end of the stage, and, right in the centre, we would
embrace; then I'd carry her graceful body off in my
outstretched arms while we declared our love for each
other ... An intensely emotional moment, all the more
acute and unhoped-for as, when I accompanied her home
or when we walked along the white sand beaches, I didn't
know what to say to my sweet stranger, I hardly dared to
lightly touch her lips. At the end of the dress rehearsal, a
lady who (I was told) was a princess – but cousin of the fat
Farouk, which spoilt my pleasure somewhat – came
solemnly to confide in me that until then her favourite
actor was Gérard Philipe, but now she wasn't so sure ...
While I sometimes wonder why my memory has retained
some pointless anecdote or other when so many eventful
phases left no trace, in this case there's no need: some
things that happen are decidedly unforgettable!

Gone now, for donkey's years, the time of tangos at
dawn, far from me the sentimental playfulness of the *Bal
des voleurs* (that's it: I've remembered the title of
Anouilh's play) and reduced to ghosts those who got their
baccalauréat in spite of themselves or became potters by
the grace of God. Finished with bread-winning jobs and
little jobs. Today my well-ordered, over-filled life no
longer leaves room for margins. And yet I do find still, but

now in order, something of what made possible that
amiable disorder in the past. I have two jobs and nothing
on earth would make me sacrifice one for the other. It
could be that, without my really intending it, there is in
this arrangement which I have constructed for myself, a
sign of caution on my part: if one doesn't put all one's
money on a single number, one indeed runs fewer risks.
Were psychoanalysis to stop interesting me or people to
stop calling on me for help, that needn't matter, I would
give more time to editing. On the face of it, the two jobs
complement each other: publishing psychoanalytic writ-
ings, trying to get an author to convey more strongly, more
rigorously, what he has been able to grasp of his
experience, doesn't contradict but on the contrary extends
my work as analyst, sometimes even gives it a fuller
meaning. One can often be drifting when one abandons
oneself simply to the stream of sessions – one can even
drown in them ... Yet I don't in fact believe that my big
analyst's chair and my small chair at Gallimard make a
pair. What I find advantageous in the co-existence of both
activities, in my professional bigamy, is that each assigns
limits to the other. Thus not all margin is lost.

One day a man came to see me, sent by a colleague
who considered an analysis appropriate for him. 'He's
very interesting, you'll see.' I found the man antipathetic from the outset, not deeply antipathetic – which
can be a good introduction, if only because one wonders
what, in the visitor or in oneself, arouses the repulsion;
no, I simply felt that if I had met that sententious,
insipid man at some social gathering or if I had known
him as a child, at school or lycée (in no way could it
have been on holiday), I would have done my utmost to

avoid him. I hadn't the least inclination to look any
further, as the sensible prescription that one go through
one's 'counter-transference reactions' with a fine-tooth-
comb would advise. He bored me stiff, that's all. How
could I spend hours listening to this garrulous pedant?
I told my colleague that he shouldn't count on me,
giving a brief motive for escaping. 'For me,' he said,
'what interests me is the neurosis, not the person.' No
doubt a little vexed by the lesson in psychoanalysis he
was giving me, I retorted too quickly: 'Well, you see,
with me it's the other way round.' Today I think we
were both wrong.

It is quite true that a neurosis, in the same way as a
dream-labyrinth or a baroque edifice, is a construction
both bizarre and precise, and that if one is too keen to
understand its tenant – for the neurosis is the landlord,
it possesses us – one runs the risk of remaining for ever
locked in it with him. But, and this is what justified my
hasty retort, I don't like the distance, so perceptible in
many accounts of analyses I have read, which insidiously transforms someone particular into Monsieur N,
the uncertain journey of a life into a neatly packaged
case-history, unexpected emotions into typical affects, a
mother, irreplaceable whoever she may be (one can't
change one's mother), into an imago. That distance also
puts one at a distance from oneself, it is first of all a
neglect of oneself. Ah, the smugness of the analyst
persuaded that, as for himself, he knows what's what
and, so far as others are concerned, they can't put one
over on him! But that's not the worst of it: the worst is
submission to a language that can go so far as to erase
the person. More distressing than the know-alls are the

devotees of the couch who, when they think they're
telling about themselves, report back the theory of
themselves they have been taught. It isn't true that if
you chase away naturalness, the unstudied, the straight-
forward, it always comes galloping back. It may trot off
and get lost in the other's words.

So, what about the two jobs? While I must have
access to both faces of reality – let's say, Freudianly,
psychic reality and external reality – it is not so that
each of them may remind me of its reverse, it is in
order to grasp *in* each of them what gives it solidity. I
need ordinary relationships and casual conversation,
various small details that punctuate the everyday. Thus
I am less likely to lose sight of the fact that being a
psychoanalyst isn't an identity, isn't a life – any more,
by the way, than being a 'patient' is. I don't have to
decide, in the daily syntax, where the main clause is,
where the parenthesis. In order to touch one reality, I
must quit another reality, break with it but know that I
shall find it again.

What I fear perhaps above all: to serve one language
only, one master only, as if I were then necessarily its
prisoner or slave. Against tyranny, there is only one
remedy: the separation of powers.

12 When was it then?

The worn image of time flowing by, of time as a
river, of time whose source is named forgetful-
ness, try as I might I can't escape it by feverishly
summoning dates, by searching for reference-points in
history; it takes hold of me again, that old image, and I
scarcely know whether it brings comfort or despair.
Must one say: times passes, or time doesn't pass? It
seems to me that both propositions flow into one
another. Only the instant − small island, or rock, clump
of trees, sandbank − is able, if it cannot interrupt the
flow, at least to give us the illusion of diverting it. The
instant, that precious wound in a time that is otherwise
doomed to indifference. But the instant creates surprise, sometimes happiness, it doesn't create memory.
Sorrow and its cry, pleasure and its tears leave no
trace. Whatever takes one outside oneself will never
later get back in but is immediately used up. The
instant needs a place, so that it isn't totally erased.

I always hesitate about going back to places I have
loved. Attracted, I approach them but, at the moment of
arrival, at the moment of touching them, I become
scared, like a criminal. So what unspeakable crime
could I be guilty of? Or else the places might
themselves be the criminals, themselves the traitors, for
having, yes, betrayed the image I had of them, an

image which ought once and for all to have revealed to
me their eternal truth. The soul of a place yields itself
immediately or never.

Our memories are cluttered. One would like only the
ephemeral to reside there, an ephemeral that memory
would have the power to make unchangeable. For in
memory — a variant, here, of the principle which
decidedly haunts me, once articulated by that pitiless
physics teacher — nothing is lost and everything is
created. At last an exception to the law of entropy! It's
always outside oneself that everything runs down. If at
night one has passionately dreamt of a woman, it is
better not to meet her the following day, not that she
necessarily appeared in the dream more beautiful,
younger or more loving than she is, but because what
she has given us in the full blaze of night, whether she
fled from or embraced us, is the secret of what in her
attracts us, no doubt *her* secret more than ours, and
something like her essence.

The gentle hinterland of Nice, the curved lines and
ochre colours of Tuscany, mineral and burning Crete,
these places which I discovered once — when was it
then? — in that slight but intense shift that we call
emotion, that will later be called happiness when
memory has transformed the fugitive moment, I do
believe I shall never return to them, for fear of losing
them, for fear that, if I visited them today, I would have
to wear mourning. Sometimes it is distance which for
me guarantees presence.

I am less afraid of returning to towns, as if *they* were
living organisms whose law it is to be transformed,
organisms that may be hurt and bruised but that remain

in spite of everything themselves. It is also because their names are more resilient. Tuscany is a painting (it's in Tuscany, I would swear, that the famous aphorism originated which made Nature an imitation of Art) and any re-touching is then an affront, an offence against eternity. But Florence shall always be Florence because Florence is first of all the name of Florence. Why is it in one's own town that changes are the most difficult to tolerate, that I inevitably perceive them as excrescences, warts, works of malicious destruction? They are destroying my town. Its name no longer protects it. In Paris I am absolutely a devotee of the past. Should a tower rise up, should the claim be made that to pull down a neighbourhood is to renovate it, should a cobbler's shop disappear in the next street, I shout murder! In London I remain a charmed passer-by.

It is Pierre G (I shan't mention his name, less out of discretion than because the bond that for a time linked us remained secret and could only be forged, intense yet tenuous, in that shared secrecy) who got me to see what the passion for places can mean. Childhood memories, said Pierre, were not his strong point. Useless looking in that direction. He didn't complain about this void, this bottomless hole at the origins of memory. Neither did he extract from it the glory of having, as it were, given birth to himself. He could only note that it was the case. He wanted me to accept the fact but, for my part, I had the feeling that, while making it possible for him to survive, it prevented him from living, without knowing exactly what I meant by that.

In fact his memory was vast, ready to welcome – no,

to register – all sorts of information: telephone
numbers, the name of a minor character in a B movie,
that of a horse which had won a race at Longchamp,
that of a Secretary of State for Industrial Development,
the address of a restaurant in the Yonne where the leek
vinaigrette is worth the detour, the classification-mark
of an old book he had looked up in the Bibliothèque
Nationale, the exact location of a statue in a small
public garden in the eighteenth arrondissement ... An
inexhaustible bank of disordered data, a facetious
computer without directions for use, a Pécuchet
deprived of his Bouvard, such was Pierre's memory.

Yet sometimes it settled, and it is then that it went
astray. It would go on visits, exploring places,
determined to capture them, to grab them like a
photographer on the look-out or like a bailiff. Pierre
would describe to me the streets where he had lived,
the rooms he had stayed in, the pattern on the
wallpaper, he would specify the dimensions of the bed,
of the window, the position of each piece of furniture,
the shape of the door-handle, and from that punctilious
inventory, that endless census that mustn't let anything
get lost, there would be born in me a poignant feeling of
absence. Pierre's rooms: the more I saw them fill with
objects, the more empty they seemed to me; the more
precise the topography, the wider the desert; the more
the map was populated with names, the more silent it
was. There were only relics, there was no one there.
And in me, bizarrely, a hole, hollowing itself out,
deepened. Never had I felt so appallingly abandoned.
Deserted, kicked out into a space that would be both
desolate and rigidly cross-ruled.

Pierre's mother had disappeared in a gas chamber. Beneath all those empty rooms which he was never done with filling, there was that room. Beneath all those names, that which has no name. Beneath all those relics, a lost mother who had left not the slightest trace. One day, when was it then?, Pierre and I managed to find words that were not remains, words that, by a miracle, reached their unknown addressee.

When was it then, that day at Boissy in the accurate light of the first summer, the children chasing one another through the tall grass, suddenly a hare leaping above the daisies, the three young women lying at the foot of the three frail birches, the fat teapot under its flowered tea-cosy, both of them brought back from England (they made me miss my plane), the men practising archery, Professor Emeritus Serge correcting the position of the chest, of the fingers, of the right leg, Wladimir more gigantic than the hare, hero of the partisan war in his own country and so afraid of wasps, and Karol, involuntarily expert in the slippage of words, solemnly suspecting, in relation to I no longer recall what political business, that he could 'sniff a mouse' in all this ('but what's so funny?'), and Yves who with his extreme, incredible, embarrassing gentleness had come to confide in me his joy at being there with us, this so luminously perfect afternoon, and who didn't know that he was soon to die.

When was it then, the same day perhaps, when we were all playing volley-ball on the lawn and when, running, I grasped not the ball in flight but one of Marie-France's breasts, the size of an orange? When

was it then, this game of love and chance that made life
so fragile, so intense, those days in the flower of the
fields, those skin-deep thin-skinned days, days when
words skimmed lightly, quick and raw?

When was it then, that night when Claire, distraught,
tipped over the paraffin lamps, when I don't know what
ardour was burning us, when she ran away and when I
found her at dawn on a bench at the station in Ermont
and I calmed her down like a child walking in its sleep
to bring her gently back to a reality she didn't want?
When was it then, that time when we didn't know what
woman we loved?

When was it then, the morning when Philippe told
me in a metallic voice that Sylvie had died and my
smiling children saw me sobbing on the stone bench,
they were looking at me, and I – I was looking at what?

It is now.

13 Non-familiar voices

T he paradox of the present moment is that it can only be grasped once it is over. Or, and this amounts almost to the same thing, when it is fiction that gives rise to it. In *La Nausée*, without trying too hard to understand it, I had liked the theory invented by Roquentin, once adventure has been discredited, of perfect moments – those small involuntary works of art, very dense and completely gratuitous, that escape from the course of things. At least we still had that. I had told myself that, with a lot of luck and a little hard work, I too would succeed in experiencing a few. And indeed in my Sartrean years, but with more hard work than luck, and always forcing it a bit, I would sometimes tell myself in more or less these words: I'm living a perfect moment! The occasion would be unreliable and varied: it could arise from listening with a girl-friend on Rue Blomet to the musicians of the *Bal nègre* as well as from reading a page of Hegel alone in my room near the Pont Neuf. Suddenly, enlightenment: the universe was held in the brassy heat of the saxophone, in the sovereign cold of the concept. Today, but I would certainly no longer call it a perfect moment for it is rather in the imperfect that I perceive depth, I find myself experiencing something equivalent when, in the course of an analytic session, words are found – and it then doesn't matter which of the two protagonists they come from – that bring about at last the fragile alliance of the perceptible and the intelligible. Then one is no longer separated from language, but secretly celebrates one's ephemeral wedding with it.

I like the fact that the word 'present' also designates a gift. But I fear that, with the passage of time, it becomes increasingly difficult for me to accept this gift. That is what I dread above all in growing old. I have known, like everyone, an age – and I did all I could to prolong it – when I was able to welcome everything offered to me. An older and, as I then saw him, over-cautious friend told me one day when he saw me pay court to some woman or other: 'It seems you're always afraid to miss an opportunity.' I can recognize the justice of those words, which hurt me and took the wind out of my uncertain sails. But I see them as a tribute today, when I no longer have that freedom or that infirmity. What do we not lose the moment we believe we have acquired our identity, when we congratulate ourselves that it has stopped floating and drifting at the mercy of encounters, at the whim of days and nights!

If I think, for example, of what reading was for me and what it represents today, I can see the change that has taken place. So much so that it is no doubt through linguistic convenience, therefore an imposture of language, that I use the same word for the wild reading of my childhood and youth and the reading, always a little too conscientious and conscious, of my fortunately belated maturity. If I had to picture the pleasure of reading, the image that would immediately come to mind would be one, both banal and mysterious, of a child lying on the floor, in half-shadow; the position he is lying in is uncomfortable, his parents are calling him for supper, he doesn't hear them, the window is wide open onto a magnificent landscape, he has his back to it, black clouds proclaim a storm. He breaks off for a minute: he notes, judging the thickness of the book, that there are only about fifty pages left before the words 'The end' and it is then that sadness furtively slips between the lines. That is because light comes from the book, because the book is both window and food, because the storm, the lightning, the waiting and the urgency are on each page and because the words 'The end' are not far from saying the end of the world, in this time when you never talk of 'taking a book', for it is the book which takes you. The happiness of being thus plunged into one's reading is all the more intense because one feels it, at the very moment when one abandons oneself to it, already imbued with a sweet melancholy. What shall we plunge into next? We shall only be able to walk on the surface of things. Cautiously. And if we ever take risks, it is because, unknown to us, fiction will have got hold of us, will have transformed us into the hero of a novel despite ourselves.

Yesterday I attended a meeting where, as is to be expected, the death of narrative was scholastically announced once more, but more as good news than as disaster. When I hear this, I am enraged. They might as well announce that childhood is dead or, more appalling, that all the children are dead and that mankind, in control of itself at last, has entrusted to computers the task of 'producing texts'! But what is a life if one doesn't recount it to oneself? And, we do know, for a single life

there are a hundred possible biographies. And, we know
too, the power of the narrative depends on its weakness,
on its faltering – on giving way, default, failure. We spend
our time inventing true accounts for ourselves, content
like professional historians to change our version of
events under the pressure of the present, without ever
being able to affirm that this is the definitive version. Or
we modify the angle of vision while affecting to forget that
it alone determines the field which the eye will encom-
pass, hiding what is left that another eye will settle on. As
long as one believes one is invoking the law of reality, one
must accept mistakes, proceed through approximations.
But when one enters into fiction, then one is constricted to
a Swiss watchmaker's precision, one is possessed by a
craze for accuracy, and even the apprentice writer that I
shall always be divines the gap between the word which
unveils the thing in naming it and the one which always
risks doing away with it. It doesn't take much when one is
writing – an image, a verb, a comma – for everything to
collapse!

When I was really immersed in my reading, the theme
of the story hardly mattered. 'That morning, in the bitter
cold, young Thomas Neumann was pacing up and down
the main street in the small town of xxx', the charm was
working straightaway. What was going to happen to
Thomas, what was going to happen to me, and where
would the event come from, the event which, like a thief,
could only appear where I didn't expect it, yet I was doing
nothing *but* expect it. It had already taken place, since
someone was narrating it, yet it was about to happen,
since there was someone who didn't know about it. And
author and reader were nothing without each other, one

no longer knew who gave the news to whom, endlessly
they exchanged places. *There* was the wonder – the ebb
and flow of the excitement lay there. While the hero of a
novel may suffer lost illusions, the reader only experi-
ences the acquiring, only the sustaining of the illusion.
He is protected from disappointment.

'That morning ...' The charm that I conjure up worked
for a long time in this way, so much so that my dearest and
most unattainable wish still is to write what is
disdainfully called a railway novel, which one starts at
Austerlitz and leaves on the seat at Angoulême, having
only skipped a few pages of description (appropriately
enough it was at the Saint-Pierre-des-Corps junction), for
the use of the next traveller, or rather female traveller, a
woman of thirty with dark eyes, wearing a fur collar and
fur hat, whom you passed on the platform and who you
could swear turned and bestowed on you a smile as she
got on the train.

Even when, having become less enamoured of novels –
and by the same token, for they go together, less
romantic,* less of a traveller, less familiar with railway-
lines, I devoted myself to the more austere experience of
works of philosophy, even then narrative remained my
way in. The day when Alquié, feeling our attention
wander, told us with the stammer which was for me the
delightful flaw in his militant rationalism: 'If one is to
believe what Descartes tells us, namely that each
Meditation follows on from the one of the day before, well
he had quite a full week!', that day was for me
consecrated bread. Thus, even meditations were inserted

* *romans* and *romanesque*.

into the everyday, metaphysics wasn't necessarily fleshless like a skeleton but carried us into a second life like a
novel, thoughts had a history. And suddenly I saw in the
'Once more, of God; that he exists' the equivalent of a
chapter title from the *Three Musketeers*, which I had read
some years earlier with the greatest excitement (Ah!
Milady baring her scarred shoulder!). All philosophy, I
told myself, is first of all the invention of a form, and that
is why I was bored to death by those who claimed only to
put forward ideas. No: Plato was a playwright; the young
Hegel had written the most exhilarating of apprentice
novels; and Hylas and Philonoüs would have bored me
stiff if I couldn't have glimpsed through their dull
dissertations the fragile grace of a duo sung on the stage of
some provincial opera house. That the word be transformed into flesh is decidedly the only thing which
interests me. The mystery of incarnation is not in my eyes
a matter of religion but of aesthetics.

The eagerness to read has stayed with me but seems to
have changed its face. It has become more impatient, it is
no longer a plunge into the deep, it has lost its power of
transfiguration. That makes me very unhappy but I can't
do anything about it. I look for the reasons for this
falling-off of what was a passion and is now no more than
an interest. I sometimes, like everyone else, blame the
surfeit of books offered to the consumer – that dizziness
which comes over us in large bookshops – or the
mediocrity (worse still, the sameness) of the 'products' on
offer. But these grievances don't work, they easily turn
into their opposite: all books are excellent, moreover each
of them finds at least one reader, why couldn't I be that
one? Then I incriminate myself and my activity as a

professional reader that forces me to assess the most disparate manuscripts, after which I feel like a wine-taster or judge of perfumes who dreams of washing with household soap and of drinking a glass of cold water. Or else I invoke my need to find myself inside my own boundaries in the evening after having been for hours as if magnetized by, sometimes even sucked into, the world of those who come to talk to me and to themselves. Be that as it may. But one might just as well say that the guilty party is this piercing concern we have for our identity, and that this concern changes with time. God knows we sought it, this identity, we suffered when it was so uncertain, so precarious, so largely dependent on some teacher, on some love or other. How shaming to recognize that it was undoubtedly constructed only of borrowings, and at the very moment when we were infatuated as never before with our uniqueness! Even today I feel slightly disturbed when I notice in what I take to be my own voice Merleau-Ponty's deep and seductive intonation. And when, irritated, I briskly crease my nostrils, my irritation increases at the thought that it's a tic which has come straight from my grandfather. My taste for fast driving and my way of holding the wheel, that's my uncle François; my fear of being disliked, that's Gilles and maybe Blackie, my efforts to ease conflicts, that's Sartre inverted, and the pleasure taken in a heated discussion on the terrace of a café is Sartre the right way up. Well, I'll stop the list — I fear too much that, seeking to define myself, I shall find among so many relics of others only a relic of myself!

It's one thing when it is just a matter of gestures or habits and they are the imprints in us of those we loved or

took for a while as models. But those we thought we were
indifferent to, those we have detested, mark us just as
much, and sometimes right inside what we consider our
most intense passions and our most definite tastes. I have
experienced this suffering: that of resembling what one
despises, harbouring in oneself what one rejects, having
one's enemy as an intimate interlocutor. If I have freed
myself from it, the merit isn't mine. It's only that a time
comes when, less anxious to discover what one really
holds to, one is satisfied with loving what holds one: those
with whom one lives and who seem to find pleasure in
one's company, work about which one no longer wonders
what its *raison d'être* is, the assurance that every day
provides something to like. Here too I shall stop the list,
fearing, this time, the insipidness of a eulogy for
measured wisdom, which everything conspires to contradict and above all, in my case, my job as analyst.

It is in this *métier*, on this loom* that weaves and
unweaves, unties and re-ties, that I now encounter what I
formerly used to look for in reading and don't any longer
find there, as if reading can no longer carry me away to
the unknown. This *métier* is the spot that, by creating a
hollow, simultaneously deepens and animates all the
other spots.

I like the fact that Freud characterized psychoanalysis
as 'ordinary conversation'. It's so easily imagined that we
collect in our antiseptic consulting-rooms frightful
confessions, blood-stained or perverse stories of crime
and sex and that, insensitive and regal, we respond to all
this passion with a few words which only we ourselves, out

---

* *métier* = 'loom' as well as 'job'.

of infatuation, and our patients, out of obligation to the transference, will consider as oracles. Ordinary conversation, yes; but not allowed for by the organization of our lives, especially not nowadays when most of our relationships are so defined that nothing happens that hasn't been prescribed in advance. An organ is the product of its function. We need very particular circumstances in order to tell and listen to the unexpected. Sometimes this happens, and some novelists testify to it – I'm thinking of Conrad –, novelists who, in a chance encounter with a stranger in the back room of a café, on a train, in some far-away port, places where one has lost one's ties and reference-points, find the impulse for a story from which they must free themselves at any price as from a burdensome secret. An ordinary conversation in a situation that isn't ordinary but that is always in danger of becoming so if ever the positions of each should freeze, no doubt this is what makes every session for me something which continues to seem absolutely strange – for very quickly one no longer knows what one is looking for nor what one expects – and at the same time something which continues to touch me in my heart of hearts. I may forget the history and the dramas, sometimes even the names of these intimate strangers with whom I have had dealings, I may have kept no trace of what sustained or tormented them, and yet they are there, continuing a bizarre existence in me which makes me wonder if I ever pass one of them in the street or a public place: did I dream about him, is it an old friend lost from sight, is it someone I don't know but have heard of from a third party and for whom I have invented this face? Who is it then, this man or this woman who comes

towards me with an embarrassed smile before moving on?
It wouldn't take much for me, at such a moment, to
believe in the reality of previous lives.

It is here that I make the link with reading. Not that I
confuse my illegible patients with books, still less with
texts for which I would be the word-processor, nor that I
equate an analysis with a piece of writing: analysis has no
author, it has no form, it has no style, and it is only by
artifice that one attributes to it, after the event, a
necessary curve. But I believe that the movement which
in the past carried me towards reading, towards the
unknown origin of those words, as if I were at last going to
find the answer to I don't know what enigma, is very close
to the movement which transports me and deports me
today towards these voices, in this other *langue*, close to
these silences from another time, another terrain. At least
I am freed from that yoke, that couple, that pair, hateful
above all others, of what is one's own and what is foreign.
Pleasure can be found in exile, when exile has been
chosen.

Have the demons of my childhood whose names were
'familiar' and 'nothing-to-say' really changed their face?
What I still dread is to be reduced to a present that
would give nothing, to a mute present – mute as an
identity-card or as a tombstone. Words kill when they
have designs on us.

14 With no other power

W ho likes renunciation? That Sartre hadn't wanted me for the rôle of 'boy' at the Casino de Paris was no reason for me not to be at the party! I gave my first articles – and to begin with, as is the custom, my first reviews – to *Les Temps Modernes*. Later, in the sixties – having become fathers, we remained boys – I belonged to the Editorial Committee. And for over fifteen years – this once I can place it in time without any effort – I've been running my own journal. It keeps me running too. With the journal I don't experience that weariness, that absence of anticipation, which can so easily permeate our days when nothing – and this can happen – sets the mind going and we suffer, though vaguely, from inertia: an inertia in which we believe we see only the reflection of dead things. It is rare for a pleasure to offer a certain constancy, to guarantee a continuity. Writing, loving, both give in this respect only one certainty: that of being doomed to the most extreme changes of mood. Friendship alone perhaps, even if it involves infatuations, is free from this disturbance. Walking also, up hill and down dale, as at each step it discovers its own rhythm, without jolts, and at the same time creates the surrounding countryside, which ends up in motion too, freed from all geography. I feel a friendship for the N.R.P. (as those who work on the *Nouvelle Revue de Psychanalyse* call it). It's my long walk in the country, my beaten track, and my converse, all of them everyday.

Unavowable pleasures aren't the only ones we find incongruous: combing manuscripts, and sometimes vigorously brushing them down, selecting the typeface and its size, correcting proofs, doing the lay-out, deciding the order of articles and the colour of the cover, chasing up the printer – I take pleasure in everything which most people balk at. And I would like it not to stop at that: I would like to set out the finished object in the bookshops, in full view to attract or hidden so as to be found, to hand it to the buyer and see what he looks like. It's only at that moment, when it has become his possession, that I would be willing to go away. It might be the same for a book that I alone would put my name to. But it so happens that it's different. A book is a piece of oneself and all of oneself in that piece. At the end of writing it, one meets shame rather than pride, mourning not joy. Quickly then out, to mingle with the passers-by, to get a paper and drink a beer, to be anyone and speak everyday words, to find again, after too long a sojourn in retreat and private idiom, the public domain. Or else to hum one of those idiotic songs that give flavour to ordinary life, perhaps because they don't belong to anyone.

To manufacture – the term suits me – a journal involves a whole series of tasks that we call modest. What gives them their apparent modesty resides in this: it is language that's rendered modest by them – language to which I have always attributed, above all when it's assertive, a natural tendency towards arrogance. Do I find in the lengthy and meticulous carrying out of these tasks, in this voluntary servitude of careful piece-work, a means of humbling the pride of words, as if I could, through my vigilant attention, through the succession of various stages of the processing they are subjected to, no longer be at their mercy, by dint of having scrutinized the material they are made of, as an anatomist scrutinizes the organs of a body or a short-sighted person the face of the loved one? To be a typographer, to be a psychoanalyst: the dream of both is to incarnate the letter, to give body to the word.

Each time an issue of the journal comes off the press, I palpate it like an obstetrician with a new-born baby: 'Not bad, this one.' Or: 'Tell me, don't you think he's got flat feet or too big a head?' And I busy myself with the next. For I like that too: that time is on my side here – *work in progress* – and that it's a collective work; it too doesn't belong to anyone, while at the same time resulting from the most singular attributes of each, from what he alone can voice in the way he does.

I said I felt a friendship for the journal. Yet there is something which doesn't altogether suit me, which is that it's advertised as a journal *of* psychoanalysis. I would prefer, at least nowadays, that it didn't have that label, not that I wish it to come forward masked or ashamed, but for other reasons. Why do we have to lean on an authority to serve as guarantor? Are we so afraid, when we speak, of being illegitimate children, without name and without recognizable identity? I trust the power of words only when that power is derived from themselves alone, when they make their fragility perceptible to me – like the beauty of a face, like that of an early spring or late autumn sky – unseasonably.

Then we experience the happiness of inventing what is. When psychoanalysis, migrant too, out of season also, manages to create the object that it contemplates, its resources are as inexhaustible as a metaphor's. It transports its passenger where he didn't think he would be going. And there it is that at last he meets himself.

It wasn't Sartre's authority that made me leave *Les Temps Modernes*. It wasn't only the ascendancy exercised by Lacan over his followers that made me keep my distance. In both cases my unease came from what I experienced as an abuse of power. But what abuse?

At *Les Temps Modernes*, Sartre could be tyrannical when the fancy took him, but he was a cheerful, debonair tyrant and soon forgot his own decrees. I had seen him, from near or far according to the epoch, take up political positions in which I didn't always recognize myself and, especially, didn't recognize him: how could he thus denounce, and with such contempt, yesterday's friend? Why this verbal violence? But a few quick steps in his company were enough for me to feel I had found again the 'boy without any collective significance, an individual by the skin of his teeth' who serves as epigraph to *La Nausée* and the man 'whom anyone is equal to' who concludes *Les Mots*. I knew that he loved writing plays, while claiming it was always on commission, and that in his private life he was an irresistible actor – but resistible martyr. So I would tell myself that politics too was for him a melodrama made to order in which, unable to be the author, he played a rôle; I thus saw his volte-faces less as repudiations than as changes of rôle. Hadn't he had great fun writing *Kean*? And then, gradually, I thought I could put my finger on what remained unchanged through the diversity of commitments and on why, every time, they became more assertive, more intransigent, more destructive: it wasn't so much action that interested Sartre as the idea of a pure agent, of an individual as free as the God he had ascribed to Descartes. But that individual could only be born of a rupture with his opposite: passivity, submission, the inert. And the liberation of the slave was to liberate the master too. A hope endlessly shattered, but always eager to rise again. Never would this small man have looked to a great man* for help, but if the active force was called French Communist Party or Fusion Group then he would go along with it for a while, before breaking off and embodying elsewhere the undiscoverable subjectivity.

When language becomes political, politics always wins and, insidiously, perverts the destiny of words by subjecting them to its own laws: to convince, to argue, to point at the adversary and reduce him to silence, never to admit to being disarmed. The philosopher, unwittingly, sometimes finds himself back inside the skin of the orator. Believing that he is still thinking, he has already yielded to a reasoning madness. What if the abuse of power, wherever it takes place, has always come from a betrayal of language, and that most insidious betrayal – the one that denies what it is doing? How can one speak in order to silence others? Certainly Sartre never imposed silence on anyone, except maybe on himself whom he never stopped fighting, as if each morning, for hygienic reasons, he had to think against himself (he made that into his

* *un grand homme.*

watchword): wanting to be 'nobody's son', he could only
beget himself by means of a continuous creation. Cause
of himself, only; never servant of a cause.

I wasn't therefore put off by his certainties, nor by
the fact that he changed them often without warning.
On the contrary, when – still at the lycée – I had read
L'Imaginaire, I'd liked the fact that he had divided his
book into two parts: a short one entitled 'What is
certain', and a longer one, 'What is probable'. I
admired his nerve, while no doubt nurturing the secret
hope that the certain might turn into the probable and
that the probable might slide, as the years went by,
towards the improbable ... Consequently the clear-cut
distinction between the real and the imaginary would
have some chance of being less radical. A disappointed
expectation: it failed to take account of Sartre's
relentlessness in wanting to grasp everything. Nothing –
on principle – must escape him. And he didn't much
care for what ran the risk of doing that: childhood, for
instance, beginning with his own, or the unconscious, or
confused emotions.

Sartre must have had a formidable trust in language to
cover innumerable sheets of paper in that manner day
after day. But in this passion, which astounded me and
sometimes froze me with terror, I could also see a distrust:
a thousand pages, ten thousand more still wouldn't do.
When language sets out to annex lands that aren't its own,
it becomes insatiable, like the great conquerors. An
empire doesn't want frontiers. While it doesn't doubt its
own strength, it nevertheless doubts its legitimacy. In the
end, Sartre may have had only one certainty, that words
are merely substitutes for actions, that all the words aren't

worth a single action, and that there is only one action worth the trouble: to create, but like a little boy playing a practical joke, nothing less than the world.

With Lacan too, language reigned, but in an altogether different way. However much he loved the goods of this world, he couldn't have written like Sartre, who didn't own anything, that he felt himself the owner of language. On the contrary, he found language everywhere at work outside, in dream and symptom, in the body and kinship, in action itself. We were subjected to the laws of language, language was the primordial Law. Caught in the 'nets of the signifier' – and we certainly were caught in the nets woven by the criss-cross threads of his discourse – we could wonder if we had any other existence than that of a phoneme. That was enough to humble any pretension to self-satisfaction, but also enough to strengthen the most tenacious of our illusions, that of being part of a universal logic. Our little miseries, all the inconsistency and shapelessness we could sense within us, acquired from this a remarkable depth; our failures to love or to think were only the perceptible traces of a 'lack of being' erected into an absolute, and that lack was itself the effect – beneficial, in the final reckoning – of our being ready to accept castration. For in the end, dispossessed of our beloved ego but acceding to the symbolic order, we gained in the exchange! When Lacan drew a diagram or graph, with letters and arrows, twists and spirals, we didn't despair, each in our corner, of finding our portrait in them, infinitely more complex – in this schematic representation – than the one reflected back to us by any old mirror, namely by all our fellow-creatures.

I overdo it here a bit because it seemed to me that
Lacan, for his part, overdid it with language, to the extent
of wanting to put it on an intangible pedestal so as to make
it even more absolute. Why did he gradually stop trusting
purely in the movement of his own words and the pauses
between them? Yet he excelled in that exercise which is
as risky as any love. But he knew, as women know even
better, that to talk is always, to a greater or lesser degree,
to chat up.* No doubt, from the first day, we have spoken
only to obtain what isn't given to us. The graphs, the
Moebius strips, were supposed, like science, to escape
from chatting up.** A matheme, *that* doesn't brag, and is
all the more impressive, like the last word.

During the final years of his life Lacan, it seems – I
didn't witness it – would remain silent in front of the
Borromean knots he drew on the blackboard; gripped in
his turn by them, he let them speak instead of him.
Could *silence* really be what would at the same time
threaten and denounce the abuse of language? The
paradox is that we commit this abuse of language to
remedy its falterings, its internal void, its violent or
sweet melancholy. We want to grant it an indisputable
authority, we foolishly expect it to have the certainty of
a thing, the presence of a body. And that is the moment
when, out of too exclusive a love, we misunderstand it
the most. For if it often comes to mind that we are for
ever separated from language, that is because language
is separation and tells only of separation. And if, while
abandoning ourselves to its powers which remain so

* *baratiner* = to shoot a line, bamboozle, hoodwink.
** *baratin* = (also) blarney, patter.

close to those of magic, we accede to an unheard-of
truth, are carried away and ravished by the beauty of
language, that is because it is the distant, insistent
echo of all our losses; it makes us go through them
again, in every direction, to the extent of having us
believe: this time, which would be the true first time,
that's it, we've got it, the thing is wholly in the words,
their trajectory comes to a stop. The poem of the
moment; a precarious, eternal marvel.

15 At the end of the line

When the high-pitched ring can be heard at that time of day, he knows it's her. He doesn't have to wait, he knows, he doesn't have the slightest hesitation. It can only be her, the telephone rings every evening at the same time, almost to the second. He imagines her staring at the small clock in her bedroom where nothing has changed for so many years, where not a single object has been moved even by a millimetre, where the photographs she no longer sees are all, in little oval frames, carefully placed on the mantelpiece: the picture of her mother with the light eyes, that of her brother in an airman's uniform, that of her two sons with the sailor-suit collars – these are the photographs taken by professionals, and there are many others that she herself took once upon a time, 'snapshots', with a Kodak box camera placed upright against her chest, and then others again that he took, but those too are ancient, twenty years, thirty years, it has been a long time since, for her, life stopped.

Here it is, it's time, he picks up the telephone, at first there's a small silence and that silence confirms, if there were any need for confirmation, that it is indeed her, he hears her voice, she says a few words, that it was very cold today or that it'll rain tomorrow or else she announces an illness, a death, François is in hospital, it's his heart,

Anne Dubac will be buried at Père-Lachaise, poor thing, or else, and it's said in the same tone, which isn't one of complaint, which isn't one of calamity: your brother waited all day for the plumber. And he, on his side, tries to give her more comforting news, that he met someone really interesting today, that the children came back from the mountains very proud of their exploits, that the hyacinths she gave him for Christmas are beginning to flower on the balcony, anything that may signify to her that life goes on, it doesn't matter what so long as it's a sign of life, but the slightest signs are undoubtedly already too much for her, since she simply wants to assure herself of his presence at the end of the line and is already asking something she knows, whether he will be in tomorrow at the same time so that, like this evening, like yesterday, like the previous weeks and months, she can reach him at that hour, which is the time when he has finished work and got back home. Sometimes all the same he's not going to be there, he'll go directly from his office to the restaurant, to the cinema, to some friends, and then, cautiously, he must tell her: 'No, tomorrow I won't be in but the day after definitely.' – 'At the same time?' – 'Yes, at the same time.' And that disturbs her, she'll call back right away to ask him: 'That's right, tomorrow?' – 'No, the day after.' – 'At the same time, quarter past eight?' 'Yes, or earlier if you'd prefer, I'll be in earlier.' That disturbs her too, she doesn't like the time to be changed, no modification must be introduced into the time-table, not the slightest modification must be introduced. Anywhere. Everything that can happen now has for her one name only: accident.

She must be in control of her call, in control of her

time. He must be there at the end of the line. It must be an absolute certainty. Now *he's* the mother.

She had been, he believed, hardly present in his life. What did she know about him? So little. Nothing. Nothing about his work, nothing about his loves, nothing about his buried sadness that she had passed on to him, he was sure of it, even less about what made him happy, which he had had to win despite her, she who had always been afraid of the future. (Like her, in the street, he walked with small steps and, as soon as he noticed it, he would change his pace, but through a deliberate decision which only underlined the imprint.) And he, what did he know about her? He had in him only an image that had scarcely moved with time. The distance between them had been immense. Or the excessive closeness, to the point of identity, but a secret identity. He didn't really know. He thought she had never moved him, never touched him and that for her it was exactly the same: he had never managed to move her, to touch her. Yes, once: she had come from Brittany, where she was living at the time, to have supper with him. He still remembers thirty years later where they had supper, Place Péreire, on a terrace. It was summer, they had turbot with mousseline sauce and wine from Bouzy. He was alone in Paris, held back by the oral part of an exam, and she had come specially for him. Thus in the course of fifty years they had had one lovers' rendezvous.

There's something odd. When he speaks about it to others, no one understands. 'What, she never asks to see you, yet she telephones you every evening. She lives far away? Abroad?' – 'No, very near. But very far also. And it's not that she doesn't ask to see me, she doesn't *want* me

to come. Stubbornly refuses. If I insist, she gets angry.
What she wants is to have me at the end of the line, at the
appointed time.'

To have me at the end of the line. In her time.

He repeats these words, he repeats them as she repeats
every evening: 'Tomorrow, I shall call you at a quarter
past eight. Will you be there?' — 'Yes, tomorrow at a
quarter past eight, I'll be there, don't worry.'

Ten years ago, she would sometimes say: 'One
shouldn't live so long. If I had the courage ...' Now she no
longer says it.

An image persists. It was another old woman, the
mother of one of his childhood friends. She stayed in
bed all day. Doctors pronounced her very weak: there
comes an age when one no longer goes to the trouble of
naming the illness. He had come to pay his respects.
She too had been active, this bedridden woman. He
had wanted to say a few words to her, to speak to her
about her son's successes, about the beauty of her
house in the autumn sun. She wasn't listening to him,
she wasn't looking at him. In front of her, at the foot of
her brass bed, a television set had been installed. Her
gaze was caught by what flashed past on the screen:
images of war in Afghanistan, a regatta at Newport, a
building in flames in the 15th arrondissement, then a
singer in sequins, and she was watching it, mute, she
was letting herself be absorbed by it, deaf, as if all
these ghostly shadows, rock stars and guerrillas
jumbled, merged, were the reality that was awaiting her
and as if these shadows were coming slowly, inexora-
bly, to seize her, to take her with them into this
intermediate world which was no longer that of the

living and already, not completely but almost, that of the dead.

Like a child, he wondered 'where does one go when one dies?' and he stole out of the big red room. He walked for a long time across hills with supple forms like the breasts of a woman, among the vines. He wanted to exorcize that vision of the bedridden old woman. He told himself that this must be what it is to die nowadays, to die gently, to die under hypnosis: without noticing it, to pass to the other side, into the screen you are no longer watching but which is watching you, which gradually absents you from the people close to you, from yourself, from memory of the world, to rejoin the anonymous insubstantiality and endless disorder of images.

She, by contrast, was vigilant, the one who telephoned him every evening to say nothing except that she would telephone him the next day. Sometimes it exasperated him: this fixed habit of an obstinate old person, this control which, without realizing it perhaps, she exercised over him. He had to be there, at his post. But exasperation soon gave way. He had to admit that he was at last extraordinarily moved. At bottom they must share the same irrational conviction: that as long as they were both there at the end of the line, the life-line would not be broken. Often, when younger, he had told himself that when she died he wouldn't experience too much grief. Now he would like to die before her. He would have taken care to plug in an answering machine on which the following message would be recorded: Yes, darling mother, you can call me tomorrow, as usual, at a quarter past eight. She would hear his voice recorded for eternity, and in her own way she, who had told him repeatedly over the years that she wasn't gifted for conversation, would be able to speak to him.

And so the whole secret between them and everything that had remained hidden inside both of them in the clumsiness of gestures, in abortive impulses, in the unease of bodies, everything that must indeed have been registered, like the message on the answering machine, but falling short of and beyond all speech, would unwind along the line, endlessly. And together they would go through a succession of rooms, of rooms whose double-locked doors would open one by one at the sound of their voices. Then they would begin the journey again several times, each time with a more supple step, and it would no longer be an interlocking of rooms but a high plateau stretching as far as the eye could see, where a slight wind would be blowing. They would stop walking once they had come to love this vast and light region of silence.

Infans scriptor

Commissioned by Robert M. Young
Edited by Selina O'Grady and Ann Scott

Typeset in 12 on 14pt Bodoni

Designed and produced for Free Association Books by
Chase Production Services, Chipping Norton, Oxon

Printed and bound in Great Britain by
T. J. Press, Padstow, Cornwall